# THE FOREST POLTERGEIST

## CLASS B ENCOUNTERS AND THE PARANORMAL

W. T. WATSON

BEYOND THE FRAY

Publishing

ISBN 13: 978-1-954528-78-9

Cover design: Disgruntled Dystopian Publications

Beyond The Fray Publishing, a division of Beyond The Fray, LLC, San Diego, CA
www.beyondthefraypublishing.com

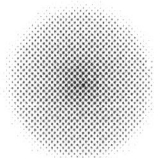

BEYOND THE FRAY

Publishing

*But there is another kind of haunting, which is still more mysterious and strange, though by no means unfrequent, and which, from the odd, sportive, mischievous nature of the disturbances created, one can scarcely reconcile to our notions of what we understand by the term ghost; for in those cases where the unseen visitant appears to be the spirit of a person deceased, we see evidences of grief, remorse, and dissatisfaction, together with, in many instances, a disposition to repeat the acts of life—or at least to simulate a repetition of them: but there is nothing sportive or mischievous, nor, except where an injunction is disobeyed or a request refused, are there generally any evidences of anger or malignity. But in the other cases alluded to, the annoyances appear rather like the tricks of a mischievous imp. I refer to what the Germans call the poltergeist, or racketing spectre, for the phenomenon is known in all countries, and has been known in all ages.*

Catherine Crowe. *The Night-Side of Nature; Or, Ghosts and Ghost Seers.* 1850.

*... The usually assumed classes of paranormal phenomena are not distinct. NDEs can occur in conjunction with UFO experiences; Big-foot has been sighted during UFO flaps; there are accounts of*

*Bigfoot making bedroom visitations. Fairies and uniformed military personnel have been encountered in ET abduction experiences. Poltergeist phenomena are found in the lives of crop circle investigators and UFO witnesses.*

Hansen, George P. *The Trickster and the Paranormal.* 2001

# CONTENTS

# INTRODUCTION

I have been fascinated by Sasquatch since I was a child. The idea of a bipedal hominid or ape of enormous size wandering the wilderness areas of the world intrigued me. The thought that a so-called "missing link" might exist, demonstrating once and for all the primacy of the theory of evolution, made me hope that some intrepid explorer would bring back incontrovertible proof that the "abominable snowman" existed. I read and enjoyed works like Ivan Sanderson's classic *Abominable Snowman, Legend Come to Life* and, a little later in my life, rooted for Steve Austin as he scrapped it on with a Sasquatch in the forests of California. I missed *The Legend of Boggy Creek* movie (strict grandparents who did not think it was appropriate), but listening to all my friends discuss it, I feel as though I did actually experience the film.

In those days, of course, no one writing about the subject regarded Sasquatch as anything more than an undiscovered animal. Theories varied, with some believing the creatures were relict hominids or, perhaps, even surviving Neanderthals, and others feeling that the Sasquatch was a member of the great ape family, a surviving species from the time when humans and animals crossed the Bering Land Bridge during the last ice age.

There was no doubt, amongst researchers of the time, that if one were to encounter a Sasquatch, one would be encountering a solid, flesh and blood creature that could be harvested or captured. Since the "experts" told me this was true, I believed it and felt certain, in my youthful enthusiasm, that it was only a matter of time before some intrepid soul brought in a Sasquatch, dead or alive, to applause and scientific acclaim.

While Sasquatch fascinated me, the Hairy One was not the only unknown that took up my attention in my elementary and then secondary school years. My father had experienced a UFO sighting in the 1950s, and his story led me to explore that subject. I had read a comic book about ghosts and so developed an interest in ghost stories and hauntings. I consumed books by people like Frank Edwards, outlining all manner of weird things that happen in our world and which science had trouble explaining.

As the result of all this reading and, later, TV shows like *In Search Of ...* and *Unsolved Mysteries*, I developed into what would now be called a Fortean. In other words, I am familiar with and interested in a wide range of phenomena that cannot be explained by the current scientific paradigm.

It was this ongoing passion for the strange that led me, in my fifties and now in my sixties, to begin writing books. I first put some of my knowledge of arcane topics to work in novel form before my publisher, Beyond the Fray, asked if I might write a book about the subject of my first novel, the phantom black dog apparition.

I had done a lot of research on the black dog and did a deeper dive into the folklore as I researched my first nonfiction piece. I published that work, *Phantom Black Dogs: Walkers of the Liminal Way*, not long after the publication of my novel. That book led to several others until eventually, I took up the Sasquatch topic in my last tome, *Sasquatch Canada: Beyond British Columbia*. In that book, I took a look at some of the hundreds of encounters with Sasquatch in the Canadian wilds (and, in at least one instance, not so wilds).

Those who have read *Sasquatch Canada* know that I chose to focus almost exclusively on eyewitness reports of the creature, what the Bigfoot Field Researchers Organization (BFRO) calls class A sightings. By themselves, these witness accounts create a great mass of anecdotal evidence for the existence of an unusual bipedal creature in the forests and even, occasionally, on the prairies of Canada.

One of the things that one notes, in reading and researching cases of visual sightings, is how pedestrian many of those incidents are. As I commented in *Sasquatch Canada*, the eyewitnesses to these creatures most often sound as though they are describing an encounter with any one of Canada's megafauna (moose, elk, bear, etc.). What sets these visual encounters apart is the astonishment of the witness upon seeing something that is not supposed to exist, an astonishment that sometimes produces other emotional reactions. It is not unusual for a witness to take some time out of the wilderness after spotting one of these creatures, for example, or to at least avoid the area where they had their encounter.

Of course, reactions to an eyewitness encounter vary across a wide spectrum. There are those experiencers who move to the other end of the scale and become obsessed with what they saw, spending all their free time in the woods, seeking to have the experience again.

I think that we can safely say, though I do not have a source for this statement, that there are more people actively engaged in the hunt for Sasquatch than there have ever been. The Hairy One has become something of a pop culture icon, and television shows and podcasts continue to feed into this interest, informing more and more people about this fascinating enigma and driving some of them to look for Sasquatch, either in an organized fashion or in a more informal manner.

Those people who are actively seeking Sasquatch are, of course, looking for the pinnacle of all Sasquatch experiences, a visual sighting, but they use a variety of, to them, obvious and telltale "signs" to tell them when they are in an "active area". I covered those signs in *Sasquatch Canada*, in the chapter that led up to this book, entitled *Forest Poltergeist*. These indicators include wood knocking, rock throwing, bipedal footsteps, strange tree structures and more.

BFRO calls such evidence a class B encounter, and it is these encounters that really make my Fortean brain hare off in a lot of different and distinctly non-physical directions. In this book, chapter 1 will be dedicated to looking at a "typical" class B encounter. We will then go on to look at a list that I compiled in *Sasquatch Canada* of the alleged signs of Sasquatch activity in an area, in the absence of visual sightings. Chapter 3 will be devoted to the genesis of this book and will propose an alternative to Sasquatch for our class B episodes: the forest poltergeist of the title. The next two sections of the text will acquaint the reader with the housebound version of the poltergeist. The discerning reader will quickly recognize considerable similarity between these hauntings and the activity associated with Sasquatch in the bush.

Once the reader has some idea what a poltergeist actually is, we will spend several chapters in a side-by-side comparison of the most common class B signs and related poltergeist activity. Amongst the related poltergeist phenomena, the reader will even find instances of tracks made by a mysterious force and a variety of vocalizations, some stunningly loud, associated with poltergeists and hauntings.

In chapter 11, I will sum up my findings to that point and then go on to spend several chapters giving some proposed answers to the question: if, indeed, the forest poltergeist exists, what is it? I will touch on everything, in these sections, from apparitions to human psychic ability to explanations based on animistic cosmology. Finally, I will conclude with my Fortean perspective of the Sasquatch phenomenon and make a case, I hope, for a less siloed approach to the topic.

As noted above, we will begin our deep dive down this rabbit hole with the presentation of some typical class B encounters. But first, I want to say a few words about the idea of proof.

One of the obsessions of the modern-day Sasquatch researcher seems to be the idea that they want to prove, to all the skeptical scientists, that Sasquatch is real. By this, the researchers mean that they wish to present to science a body for dissection or a live specimen for close examination. While most researchers are convinced, either because of their own experiences or the experiences of others, that their subject is real, they feel driven to prove it to a scientific establishment that has no space in its paradigm for such a creature to exist.

This obsession with presenting evidence to science has been a source of never-ending frustration to the Sasquatch researchers. Despite the mass of sighting reports and physical evidence like tracks, sound recordings, pictures, video recordings and even the occasional DNA sample, the best that can be said is that some scientists are willing to risk their careers and reputations to take a harder look at the evidence. The prize of being the one to prove that Sasquatch exists has yet to be claimed.

But, the Sasquatch researchers cry, all those people are seeing something! This is a statement with which I absolutely, 100% agree. People in the wilds of North America are seeing and experiencing "something". Where I do not agree is with the idea that this leads inexorably to a giant bipedal primate playing hide-and-seek with us in the bush.

Canada, where I live, could certainly host such a creature. The wood bison, the largest land animal in North America (by weight), was thought extinct until it was rediscovered in the wilds of Canada. But I do not make the jump to assuming that Sasquatch is a biological entity simply because it could exist.

Human perception is an odd thing. I can look at a piece of cloth and say that it is green, and my spouse can look at the same piece and tell me it is blue. Which of us is right? The answer is that we are both correct, within the limits of our own perception. Perception is everything in Sasquatch cases, particularly when we dive into the experiences that BFRO have tagged as class B encounters. What to the Sasquatch researcher seems to be evidence of the presence of the Hairy One, to the Fortean opens a whole realm of possibilities.

Let's look now at some class B encounters and then open the door for a Fortean deep dive into this phenomenon.

# 1

# WHAT IS A CLASS B ENCOUNTER?

I TALK EXTENSIVELY about the *MonsterQuest* episode "Sasquatch Attacks" and producer Doug Hajicek's strange encounters at the Snelgrove Lake site in *Sasquatch Canada*. To recap, Snelgrove Lake is a remote site accessible only by float-plane in the midst of the wilds of Ontario. Campers in the area had reported sightings of Sasquatch, and the cabin where the *MonsterQuest* crew stayed had been ransacked sometime before the episode was filmed. Video taken for insurance purposes was reviewed by an expert on bears, who concluded that the damage was most likely not done by bears.

In addition, the owner of the cabin had placed a bear deterrent outside the front door—a board with screws driven through it— and something had stepped on the board, leaving traces of blood, hair and tissue behind. *MonsterQuest* brought in a team, including noted Sasquatch track researcher Dr. Jeff Meldrum, to examine the board and try to get further evidence of the presence of the Hairy One in the dense forest surrounding the fishing cabin.

Most of the episode is taken up with various items of evidence, including the blood, hair and tissue samples taken from the bear-deterrent board, but there is a classic class B incident at the end of that first episode that will serve as a jumping off point for our discussion. According to what we see on the *MonsterQuest* show and Doug Hajicek's own discussion of the incident on Wes Germer's *Sasquatch Chronicles* blog and podcast, on the last night of the team's stay, one of the crew stepped out onto the front porch to urinate.

As this individual was doing his business, a rock came sailing out of the brush and struck nearby. The crew member picked the rock up and threw it back into the forest. This action set off a series of stone throws, which caused the *MonsterQuest* team to tuck up inside the cabin. One brave cameraman (or perhaps the low person on the totem pole) remained outside, scanning the surrounding forest with both night-vision and thermal cameras to no avail.

The stone thrower was never caught, and as usually happens in these cases, Sasquatch was cautiously credited with this mischief. It seemed obvious to all involved that something with hands had to be throwing the stones. There were no humans, other than themselves, for many kilometres in any direction, so it seemed logical to assume that the only other type of being with hands in those woods was Sasquatch.

While the *MonsterQuest* incident was a very typical class B encounter, Sasquatch have been credited with all manner of disturbances in the woods.

As I am interested in Canadian cases, I refer you to BFRO report #55604, which comes to us from the Black Stone Gap area of central Alberta. A pair of bow hunters were camped for the night and, as they began to cook dinner, noted noises in the tree line some twenty-five yards from where they sat. Thinking that there might be a bear around, the two armed themselves with shotguns and continued about their business.

The noises continued, and after waiting thirty minutes, one of the hunters fired a round into the air to frighten the "bear" away. Twenty seconds later, a rock "the size of a soccer ball" flew from the trees and landed near the party, and something began to "violently" shake a nearby tree. More stones followed so that, over the course of about twenty minutes, seventeen rocks were hurled at the campers.

Deciding that discretion was the better part of valor, the two hunters packed up camp and left the scene to the mystery rock throwers. The reporting party commented that he knew bears could shake trees, but no bear could possibly throw a rock twenty-five yards. As we see so often in unexplained cases, the hunter who made the report stated that, after this frightening incident, he was hesitant about returning to what had been a favorite hunting spot.

Rock throwing is not the only behavior attributed to Sasquatch in class B incidents. BFRO report #16944 gives us an interesting account from a hunter in Ontario, on the northern border of the massive Algonquin Provincial Park. The hunting group were out for either deer or bear and, after arriving at camp, setting up tree stands and placing bait, the group retired for the night.

The next morning, as hunters will do, the witness was up very early and in his tree stand, bow in hand, waiting upon his prey. As we frequently see in these types of incidents, the hunter's first intimation that something unusual was happening came when the forest went silent around him. As he put it, "no birds, no chipmunks, nothing, and I felt as though I were being watched".

The visceral reaction continued as the witness described the hair standing up on the back of his neck and a feeling of irrational fear that prompted him to want to flee the stand and, indeed, the entire area. This deep-seated terror remained with him for about five minutes, and he was about to abandon his position when the first wood knock sounded.

The knocking came in bursts of four or five sounds and seemed to be coming from multiple locations. The reporting party, who describes himself as six feet four inches and 290 lbs, stated unequivocally that there was no way that he could have hit two pieces of wood together hard enough to make the sounds that he heard.

The hunter got out of the area and returned to the campsite. When his friends returned, about an hour later, he asked if they had heard the knocks. They responded that they had heard them but that they were quite faint since the other hunters were some distance away, having decided to stay well apart from each other.

The witness goes on to relate that, the summer before this report, he had another mysterious encounter with the phantom of the woods. In that instance, the hunter heard bipedal footsteps walking by his tent at about 0100 hours while on a summer camping trip. He noted that there were other people camping in the area, but for them to have been walking about, they would have needed to be able to see in almost complete darkness. In other words, he saw no flashlights, and when he opened the tent flap to see who it might be, he could see absolutely nothing.

Eventually, the footsteps walked off into the distance, to the witness' immense relief. He also noted a "faint skunk smell" in the area during the encounter.

In BFRO report #15419, a witness near Osoyoos, British Columbia, relates similar, mysterious activity. The reporting party was out shooting pictures at an abandoned set of log structures on a cool winter afternoon. The witness reported that it was a clear winter day and that he was using the lighting to good effect, getting some interesting pictures, when he began to feel that he was not alone. The subject had seen wildlife in the area —coyotes, moose, deer and the occasional bear—but the aspen forest was so thick that it was difficult to see into.

The witness shrugged his "being watched" sensation off as nerves and continued to shoot pictures.

As the photographer finished shooting for the day and headed for his truck, about five hundred yards away, he again had the feeling of being watched. The snow was knee deep, and he was making slow progress back to his vehicle when he began to hear twigs snapping at a range he estimated at one hundred fifty yards. The witness picked up his pace, afraid that he might be about to encounter a bear.

At this point the sounds resolved themselves into very discernible footsteps that seemed to clearly be following the photographer. The maker of the sounds was invisible in the thick cover as the witness made a dash for his truck in the rapidly fading light.

Fortunately, the witness was in the habit of leaving his keys in the truck when he came to this location. By the time he got to his vehicle, the following footsteps had closed to about two hundred feet, and the witness could hear a deep grunting sound, "like an elk, but much deeper". The photographer started his vehicle up and wheeled it around in the snow, headlights on the tree line where the sounds had been coming from. He could see trees shaking in the wood line as he made his way rapidly away from the site.

This experiencer did go back to the scene a couple of weeks later and noted in his report that he found several six-inch saplings snapped off in the general area of his experience. As there had been more the two feet of snow at the four-thousand-two-hundred-foot elevation, he was unable to find any other sign of the mysterious walker in the woods.

It is clear that the people in these reports were experiencing something. Sasquatch researchers believe that the something is a giant bipedal hominid or ape and, according to Dr. Jeff Meldrum, whom we referenced earlier, these class B signs are behaviours also seen in the great apes.

Dr. D. Jeffrey Meldrum comes with an impressive set of credentials. The good doctor has undergraduate degrees in zoology with an emphasis in anatomy and physiology, and his doctorate, from the State University of New York (Stony Brook) is in anatomical sciences with an emphasis in physical anthropology. He is a full professor of anatomy and anthropology at Idaho State University and has contributed to many volumes and papers on bipedal locomotion including *From Biped to Strider: The Emergence of Modern Human Walking, Running, and Resource Transport*. Dr. Meldrum has been interested in Sasquatch and particularly Sasquatch tracks for many years.

In his book, *Sasquatch: Legend Meet Science*, Meldrum outlines a number of behaviours attributed to Sasquatch in class B encounters that have been seen in apes.

**Stone throwing**: Dr. Meldrum notes that this behaviour is a very common element of chimpanzee aggression. The scientist then goes on to extend this to other objects, citing a field report from researcher John Mionczynski in which he was pelted by pine cones by an unseen thrower.

**Tree Shaking**: Dr. Meldrum compares this and loud vocals (which we will discuss later) along with observed chest beating to "similar antics in great apes". The anthropologist also goes on to note that biologist Birute Gablikas observed an orangutan pushing over a tree in the direction of an intruder (in this instance, herself).

**Wood Knocking**: Meldrum notes that he knows of no direct observation of a Sasquatch engaging in this behaviour but goes on to state that chimpanzees, because they split into groups to forage, use knocks to maintain communication with other foraging groups and, apparently, to relay their position. Additionally, gorillas use ground slapping for similar reasons, and a female silverback was observed to clap her hands together to attract a male's attention to a possible issue nearby (an observer). Further, Meldrum notes that slapping of the ground, trees or chest is a clear intimidation behaviour.

**"Skunky" scent**: In both visual sightings and the incidents that we are referring to as class B, a distinct smell is sometimes noted. Dr. Meldrum states that well-known Sasquatch author John Green's research and subsequent database found that the smell was reported about ten percent of the time. In the Canadian sources that I explored for *Sasquatch Canada*, my personal favourite description of the scent was that of a witness that said that the Sasquatch he sighted smelled like a wet puppy that had been rolling in garbage for a week.

Dr. Meldrum observes that gorillas have well developed axillary glands that discharge a strong musky smell when the animal feels fear or is threatened. Dian Fossey reported this scent in an incident where a silverback charged her.

Dr. Meldrum makes some other observations about ape behaviour that are germane to our discussion and which we will speak of in later sections of the book. For now, however, I would like to note that a class B episode is, by its nature, an incident in which the witness did not see the source of the mischief inflicted on them. The assumption is that the perpetrator was a Sasquatch (or more than one Hairy One), but we all know what happens when we assume something to be true.

Before I come to my alternate theory of what may be going on in the woods, let's talk a little more about some other common markers associated with Sasquatch and the logic behind that association.

# 2

# SASQUATCH "SIGN"

IN *SASQUATCH CANADA*, I outlined a number of indications of Sasquatch presence in an area. We have talked about some of those suggesters of Sasquatch activity in the previous section, but let's recap some of the others so that we can take them into consideration in the later sections of the book. We have already seen evidence in some of the introductory encounters in chapter 1.

Here is part of a list that I compiled in my research for *Sasquatch Canada* along with some additional commentary based on the foregoing chapter. The numbers do not match those in *Sasquatch Canada*, as I am consolidating some of the items for the sake of conciseness.

1. **The Silence**: Witnesses and investigators often note that the surrounding woodland becomes eerily quiet in the presence of Sasquatch. We saw an example of this phenomenon in BFRO report #16944 where the bow hunter testified that the woods went entirely silent around him as his experience got underway. I have not

seen any real explanation of this indicator of Sasquatch activity other than the assumption that the wilderness is going quiet in the presence of an alpha predator. This could certainly be the case, but given the weirdness that often ensues after this silence settles, I think we also need to look at other causes for this preternatural quiet. For example, UFO researcher Jenny Randles noted this unnatural silence as a precursor to a UFO event in what she called the Oz Factor.

2. **Sounds of movement in the brush**: Witnesses often believe that a deer, elk, or moose is about to emerge. Sometimes, this phenomenon then yields a visual sighting, while at other times nothing is seen. We saw this Sasquatch signal in BFRO report #55604 where the hunters were alerted to the presence of something in the bush by sounds of movement. Rock throwing began after an aggressive display by one of the hunters. Apparently, firing a shotgun to scare off whatever is lurking nearby can result in a stone-throwing incident with stones large enough to do some damage should they hit their target.

3. **Heavy, supposedly bipedal footsteps**: It is a common statement amongst experiencers that they can tell the difference between the sound of a quadruped and a biped walking. Again, though footsteps may be a precursor to a visual sighting, these sounds are often the only evidence that something was there. The witness in BFRO report #16944 also reported an incident of bipedal footsteps around his tent in the summer before the main incident he was reporting. The witness was very adamant that, if this was a person, they had the ability to see and navigate safely

in near complete darkness. Since most campers are not equipped with expensive night-vision gear, it seems clear that something odd was happening.

4. **Structures and creation of "nests" on the ground and suspension of items in trees:** In some reports, lodge pole pines and trees are found bent, uprooted, or stacked in patterns such as woven or crisscross configurations. In addition, researchers in certain areas have reported what appear to be nests, sized to a very large animal. Finally, in one article for a publication called *Mountain Outlaw*, the writer tells of people "finding deer carcasses suspended at height in the local woodland".

In regard to the so-called structures found in areas where the Hairy One has been seen, researchers have theorized that these structures may represent shelters, in some cases, or territorial markers. As we've seen, great apes, specifically orangutangs, will push down trees as a threat display, but I've not run across any writings about great apes building shelters.

Instead, the scientists, when they speak of great ape structures, are referring to the ground or tree nests that great apes build, which, to my eye, look rather like large bird nests. Some researchers feel that massive depressions and arrangements of grasses and other detritus on the ground constitute proof of nesting Sasquatch in the area. It is certainly true that the great apes build such nests, and, in fact, scientists are quite interested in the "architecture" of chimpanzee nests, which are built high up in trees each night.

The mention of prey animals, specifically deer carcasses, being found hanging in high tree branches is indeed mysterious. None of the predators indigenous to North America are known to engage in the stowing of kills in trees. This is, instead, a behaviour noted amongst leopards in Africa, so unless North America has developed its own unseen leopard population, or the alien big cats are taking a run at Sasquatch territory, this indicator of Sasquatch activity must remain a mystery as well. It should be noted that caching prey is not a behaviour typical of primates.

I have specifically not mentioned vocalizations and footprints since I will be dealing with those in separate sections of the book.

I have said, both in my books and on numerous podcasts and even some radio appearances, that I do not rule out the possibility of a relict hominid or unknown bipedal great ape inhabiting the wilderness of North America. Canada, for example, is the second-largest country in the world, but the vast majority of its population lives within one hundred and fifty miles of the US border. That leaves huge swathes of territory where no human being lives and very few humans venture.

If such a creature does exist, it certainly might leave behind some or all the signs that we have covered in the past two chapters, and if such an animal exists, it could be responsible for the many types of vocalizations put forward as evidence of its existence and for the massive footprints seen in many places throughout North America and the world.

The problem that I see with this assumption, though, is that, in order to credit it, we have to gift this animal with evolutionary advantages on an almost supernatural level for it to remain undiscovered for so long. The researchers who believe Sasquatch is a flesh and blood creature are convinced, for example, that these animals are extremely intelligent. This concept would seem self-evident, given their success in avoiding humans, but if it is true, then why do the creatures so often seem to blunder into sightings.

In my unscientific survey of the phenomenon, it seems that one of the most common sightings of a Sasquatch happens on or near a road. Person X will be driving along a road or highway in his or her vehicle, and a Sasquatch will walk out of the woods and either pace along beside the road for a distance or actually cross the road in front of the oncoming vehicle, sometimes at distances so close that people claim to have to slam on the brakes to keep from hitting the animal.

Such behaviour is, in my opinion, not indicative of high-level intelligence. A human, seeking to evade others of its species, would simply wait for the vehicle to pass or find some other way of arriving at his or her destination without crossing a travelled (sometimes heavily travelled) roadway or walking next to said roadway. In many cases, it almost seems as if the Sasquatch is not aware of the vehicle at all and is going about its business as it sees fit.

Following on that thought, researchers who view the Sasquatch as something other than a flesh and blood creature suggest that the creatures may be interdimensional beings of some sort, and that the Sasquatch may be going about its business because it is slightly out of phase with our reality and is not even aware of the vehicle that has spotted it.

While this might seem to some to be wild conjecture, modern quantum physics certainly leaves open the possibility of there being many dimensions. Who knows what might exist in those dimensions?

Another good example of this phenomenon is the case of the vanishing Sasquatch. I include a couple of stories in *Sasquatch*

*Canada* of a creature appearing before a person and then simply vanishing in front of them. Here is an account from *Sasquatch Canada* that is simply hard to explain.

---

In the summer of 2010, here in Whitehorse, a gentleman friend of mine was driving downtown on Azure Road to do some shopping when he noticed something walking on the right-hand side ditch. He slowed down and observed a Sasquatch two metres (seven-to-eight feet) tall walking in a southern direction at a slow, dedicated pace. He slowed down his car and followed the Sasquatch for a distance of some 30 metres.

The Sasquatch did not even look at him and seemed not to notice the car only two meters beside him and paid no attention to it. The Sasquatch acted like a man on a mission, not paying attention to anything else at all. Some five metres before a utility pole the Sasquatch started losing its overall shape, becoming gradually transparent to the point, as the witness stated to me on many occasions, that the witness could see right through it, yet its overall form was still outlining his transparent body, as the Sasquatch reached the utility pole, he totally disappeared from sight.

---

Now, obviously this is not the sort of thing that a flesh and blood creature is capable of, so the researchers who want Sasquatch to be an undiscovered animal seek to come up with explanations for these stories. One of the favourites is something called infrasound.

Referring back to Dr. Meldrum, we discover that infrasound is an ability to make extremely low-frequency sounds that a human could not hear. These sounds are used by animals for a variety of purposes. Elephants use low-frequency sounds to communicate over distances as far as thirty kilometres, for example, and tigers use the sounds to freeze prey. These ultra-low-frequency sounds are less susceptible to interference, from trees, for example, or attenuation over long distances.

Both Dr. Meldrum and *The Locals* author Thom Powell note that infrasound used on human beings produces some of the effects that we saw in our class B incidents earlier. The two authors list such effects as disorientation, uneasiness, fear, hair standing on end, dizziness and more. Powell, who encountered several vanishing Sasquatch reports in his fieldwork, theorized that the Sasquatch were using infrasound to cloud the witness' mind and then slip away into the forest while the disturbed human tried to get their thoughts back together.

While, again, I have never ruled out the physical Sasquatch and such a massive animal certainly could use infrasound, I don't feel that the infrasound "explanation" holds for cases like the one above. The witness in this case clearly saw the creature and then watched it fade from view. The driver of that vehicle reported no deleterious effects on consciousness; they simply saw a Sasquatch and watched it fade out in plain view and in broad daylight.

Infrasound will also not explain the case of a woman in Uniontown, Pennsylvania, reported by Stan Gordon in his book *Silent Invasion*. The experiencer was watching television of an evening when she heard a sound on her front porch. Thinking that it might be the feral dogs that plagued her neighbourhood, the women grabbed her shotgun and moved out the front door onto her porch.

You can imagine her horror when she discovered a seven-plus-foot-tall Sasquatch standing on her front porch. When the creature raised an arm, she assumed she was being attacked and blasted the animal with her shotgun. The creature vanished in a flash of light, leaving a very confused woman to report to Stan Gordon's group.

Again, we see no reported break in consciousness. The woman simply walked out onto her porch, felt threatened by an out-of-place animal, and shot at it to good, if puzzling effect. It's hard to see how infrasound would have played into this incident. The woman was not confused about firing a shot, and her son, who lived nearby, heard the gunfire and came running.

These two examples should suffice to place some doubt about the flesh and blood theory as the **only** theory to explain Sasquatch sightings and class B incidents. For those interested in a more complete rundown of Sasquatch as something Other, please see the work of Tim Renner and Joshua Cutchin. Their *Where the Footprints End* series is the definitive statement on that side of the argument, in my humble opinion. You'll also find a quick examination of some strange cases (Sasquatch with glowing eyes, Sasquatch practicing psychic communication and more) in my book *Sasquatch Canada.*

I'm still open to the idea that a relict hominid or bipedal great ape could be roaming the interior of Canada or other wild places. After all, Canada lost the wood buffalo for several decades, believing it to be extinct, only to rediscover it in the deep forest of Western Canada in the 1950s. I think that, instead of making "I believe this, and I am right, and everyone else is wrong" silos, we need to take a more Fortean view of

Sasquatch and say, yes, Sasquatch could be an undiscovered animal, **but** it could also be something else or perhaps even several somethings.

Let's take some time now to introduce a character who is going to trod through the rest of the pages of this book.

# 3
## THE FOREST POLTERGEIST

MY TIME for consuming paranormal media is very limited, but when I do have a chance to listen to a podcast, Seriah Azkath's *Where Did the Road Go?* is one of my go-to casts. I've been on the podcast myself with each of my books since *Mysteries in the Mist* and have always found Seriah to be a great interviewer. I owe the origin of this book to him and his sometimes cohorts in crime, Timothy Renner, of the *Strange Familiars* podcast, and Joshua Cutchin, author of several fascinating books on various paranormal subjects.

It was on *Where Did the Road Go?* that I first heard Seriah say that, if we took all the indicators that researchers took to be Sasquatch presence in the wilderness and placed them inside someone's home, we would have a poltergeist case. Seriah, Tim, and Joshua then started to refer to this idea as the wilderness poltergeist.

I was intrigued by this concept when I first heard the idea. Ghost hunting is an area of interest for me but not one that I have spent a lot of time researching. I filed the idea away in the back of my mind, knowing that one of these days I would write something on the subject of Sasquatch and resolving that I would find a way to bring the subject up in a book on that topic. I did that in the chapter titled "Forest Poltergeist" in *Sasquatch Canada*, but that brief foray into the strange world of the poltergeist simply whetted my appetite.

I decided that once my Sasquatch book was launched, I would pursue the forest poltergeist idea further. This book and its wild plunge down the rabbit hole is the result of that pursuit.

I've spent the last couple of chapters outlining what a class B incident is in the Sasquatch world and some of the strange things that have been associated with Sasquatch presence in the wilds. As I said earlier, I will deal with the subject of vocalizations and footprints in later chapters. What I want to do now is slip out of the silo of Sasquatch research and into the broader role of a Fortean investigator. When you take a look at the broader paranormal world, it becomes clear that Seriah Azkath is onto something. A class B Sasquatch episode has a lot in common with the "noisy spirit" that causes the havoc of a poltergeist case.

Before we outline a poltergeist case, let's talk a little bit about what a poltergeist is. The word, as I've mentioned, comes from the German and means something like "a noisy spirit or ghost". Tom Ogden, the author of *The Complete Idiot's Guide to Ghosts and Hauntings*, a book I turned to in my initial foray into the subject, sees a poltergeist haunting as defined by physical disturbances. While the people in such a case may have some of the typical indicators of a more traditional haunting—such as cold spots, odours, a feeling of being watched, pets acting strangely and even apparitions—there is also a distinctly physical quality to the haunting.

As Ogden puts it, "poltergeist activities include thumping and bangings, moving objects, stone throwing and starting fires". Also documented have been disturbances like ringing bells, thrown objects changing course in midair, passage of solid objects through walls, and even the observation of some witnesses that thrown objects were warm to the touch when picked up.

Rupert Matthews, in his book *Poltergeists and Other Hauntings*, looked at a number of poltergeist cases and developed a theory of the progression of these episodes. In Matthews' theory, the beginning of a poltergeist event can be so subtle that the people in the home do not perceive anything supernatural or odd about the event. Typically, the subtle sounds of an awakening poltergeist are likened to the scurrying of small animals in the walls, and often the householders seek a mundane solution to the noises, calling in repair people or pest control.

Once the household has adapted to these smaller sounds, the poltergeist seems to up the ante. Louder sounds appear, the most characteristic of which is a rapping or knocking noise and sounds that we will discuss in depth later in the book. Additionally, there may be noises like bangs or explosions.

The poltergeist progression continues, in Matthews' theory, with the movement of objects. During this phase of the event, we see all manner of objects moving in the home and objects, including local stones, actually being thrown at the experiencers. In my own research, I have seen that this is the stage in which destruction is often wrought in a home, with many breakable objects being shattered.

The destruction phase of poltergeist activity may coincide with another, very spooky aspect of the poltergeist phenomenon— apports and dis-apports. In other words, objects may simply appear, seemingly from thin air, or an object may disappear and then reappear in an unlikely or curious place. In one case I looked at for my research, the poltergeist delighted in swiping eggs from the refrigerator and then making them explode in the kitchen. The mother of the family put the eggs underneath a crate and sat on it, only to have eggs exploding in the kitchen anyway. When she checked the eggs under the crate, there were eggs missing from her little stash.

The fifth stage of Matthew's progression has to do with communication. In some, but not all instances, the "spirit" responsible for the haunting communicates with the household. This communication often takes the very basic form of raps in response to questions, one for yes, two for no, for example. On occasion, a poltergeist seems to learn speech. When this happens, it is apparent that the energy's primary desire is to shock people. "It" uses foul language and makes shocking claims about the people in the household, amongst other mischievous behaviours.

The last stages of a poltergeist event, according to Matthews, are the climax, decline and ending of the event. In other words, the disturbance reaches a peak where the activity becomes quite frenetic and then drops off until it finally ceases. Poltergeist activity may vary in time from a few weeks to a year or more.

While a "normal" haunting can be frightening to the uninitiated, poltergeist activity can be scary to even the most skeptical observer. Who wouldn't be a little put off by an unseen force capable of moving heavy objects, throwing things through the air at considerable velocity and, in extreme cases, physical attacks on the persons who live or work at the activity site. More than one researcher has noted that, if some of the objects that whiz around a poltergeist site were to hit a person, they would cause serious bodily harm. Oddly, in instances where objects in a poltergeist incursion do strike someone, they do not seem to cause serious harm. Nevertheless, poltergeist activity is known to drive people from their homes, sometimes on a temporary basis and sometimes permanently.

We do not really know what a Sasquatch is, and likewise, the source of poltergeist phenomenon is unknown. Of course, there are theories about what causes the activity. Perhaps the most commonly proposed theory revolves around the presence, in a number of poltergeist cases, of what parapsychologists call a focus, usually a child or young adult, around whom the activity seems to centre.

The focus theory proposes that, because of various stressors in their lives, some of these young people are capable of having what parapsychologist Lloyd Auerbach calls a "psychic temper tantrum". In other words, the focus sublimates his or her stress, and that stress manifests itself as outbursts of psychokinetic activity.

Another famous parapsychologist, William Roll, has given these outbursts a name. He calls them RSPK, random spontaneous psychokinesis. I have my doubts that RSPK is the one and only true source of poltergeist activity, but it could certainly get the ball rolling. I will be speaking later about some other theories of the poltergeist and my own, animistic viewpoint of the phenomenon.

So, what does a poltergeist case look like? Honestly, in my research, I have seen many different manifestations of this interesting phenomenon, ranging from the classic "things that go bump in the night" to a poltergeist that seemed to bite.

Let us start with a fairly short account of a poltergeist incident that happened at 37 Westgate Street in Gloucester, UK. Michele Eve, of the *Mystical Times* blog, gives us a concise account of this incident for our consideration.

In the late 1980s, the address was the site of the Anglian Windows company. The first sign of something strange happening in the building occurred during a business meeting where no less than eight witnesses noted the carpet rising up, on its own, in the corner of the room. Unable to explain what they had seen, the witnesses tried to ignore this bizarre event and made a joke of it.

As we will see in other cases, the carpet incident was just the beginning of a series of occurrences that defied explanation. Shortly after the business meeting, people in the building began noticing an acrid odour that was so offensive that professionals were called in to try to determine the source. No cause could be found for the smell, nor could anyone explain the presence of a large "damp patch of congealed liquid" that manifested on the ceiling.

The activity escalated further. Lights would go on and off though it is not clear whether this was caused by manipulation of the light switches or an unknown electrical effect. The office manager, Jean Brown, reported seeing the flush handles on the toilet moving of their own accord. Unlocked doors would be found locked and vice versa. Ms. Brown found herself locked in a toilet on one occasion when she went to investigate a strange noise.

The manifestations were spooky enough to drive a tenant who lived above the business out of the building. One of the young women who worked for the business called her sister to pick her up after working some overtime. It was about 2100 hours when the sister arrived, and, when the worker's sibling came into the showroom, she saw a figure in a "long robe with white hair" standing behind the sister whom she had come to retrieve.

After a scream from the driver, both sisters ran from the premises, and the worker never returned. She refused to enter the building again and went on to find other employment.

Oddly, while the one employee did depart, most of the other workers simply found the disturbances annoying. After a hand basin, which had been left propped against a door, fell down two flights of stairs without any apparent reason, the owners of the building contacted the Gloucester Cathedral to see if the building could be exorcised. The article is silent about the reply of the cathedral, but it does seem that a medium came in and performed a seance at the site.

The medium reported that he had contacted a spirit wearing a long, grey robe who informed him that he (the spirit) had committed suicide by falling from the building and breaking his neck. It was this spirit and its anger that were causing the activity at Anglian Windows, and the medium assured the building occupants that he had negotiated with the spirit, and things would calm down.

As we will see in other cases, efforts to calm a poltergeist often backfire. The new branch manager for the business was plagued by strange noises in the building, and Jean Brown, the office manager, who had been annoyed by the activity before, now found herself reluctant to go up to the second floor.

One of the standout events in this parade of activity happened after the medium's attempted intervention. A cafe owner, Jeff

Pugh, who had his business in a building adjacent to Anglian Windows, heard a loud crash, followed by the sound of breaking glass. He ran over to the Anglian Windows building and, along with the office manager, Jean Brown, rushed up to the third floor of the building. The two entered a room that had been locked to find that a heavy double wardrobe had been pushed several feet across the floor, where it had broken the window out.

The medium returned and, again, stated that he had placated the spirit haunting the building. At the same time, the cafe owner, Jeff Pugh, and a friend who was a local hairdresser decided that it would be great fun to hold a vigil in the building over Halloween night as a charity fundraising event. The medium warned against this event, but the duo decided to go ahead. Although the two did manage to raise four hundred pounds for their designated charity, they did so at the expense of spending a very unsettled night in the building.

During the course of the vigil, the radio station that was recording the event placed equipment in a locked room upstairs, only to find the equipment scattered all over the room when they went to retrieve it. The transmitter had been overturned, and wires and batteries had been disconnected. The radio station might have pulled out at this point but decided to go forward given the late hour.

The activity continued with several "bumps, bangs, and crashes" being recorded over the course of the night. The lights flickered on and off, and at around 0200, a table crashed to the floor. Fortunately, no one was injured in all the activity, and the money raised gave a semi-happy ending to the story.

The 37 Westgate poltergeist activity went on for about a year, and then, as mysteriously as it appeared, it ceased. Ms. Eve was not able to find reports of any other disturbance in that building after the one poltergeist incursion.

Now, at first blush, one might look at this story and think: what has this to do with Sasquatch? My answer would be: not a thing, but there are aspects of this story that slot neatly into the class B incidents that we have examined. The reader will note that, along with the blatant psychokinetic activity in the building (lifting carpets and sliding wardrobes), one of the first manifestations of the event was an acrid odour that was so pungent professionals were called in to try to determine the source.

As we noted in previous chapters, one of the markers of Sasquatch presence in the wilds is a peculiarly pungent, skunk-like odour that has given the creatures the moniker "skunk ape" in the Florida area. We will see, in other cases later, poltergeists producing a number of different kinds of odours, ranging from the pleasant to the very unpleasant.

The reader will also note that a variety of different sounds accompanied the 37 Westgate haunting. Described variously as thumps, bumps, bangs, crashes and so forth, these sounds are not a far cry from that most well-known pointer to Sasquatch presence, the wood knock. In cases that we will look at later, we will see cases where a clear knocking sound is heard in a poltergeist case.

Note too, that as the activity escalated, it seemed to take on a form; in the 37 Westgate case, that form was of a robed figure with white hair and a beard. Class B incidents, by their nature, do not involve a sighting of Sasquatch, but there are plenty of visual sightings that begin with the noted signs of Sasquatch presence, such as wood knocks, movement in the brush, vocalizations and so on. After looking at just one poltergeist case, we cannot draw many conclusions, but this pattern of activity culminating in the sighting of **something**, whether an apparition in a home or Sasquatch in the woods, is a commonality that we cannot ignore. Again, I will dig more deeply into this idea as we go on.

For now, however, let's take a look at two classic poltergeist cases so that we can get a better feel for this phenomenon.

# 4

## OLIVE HILL, KENTUCKY

WHEN YOU MENTION the poltergeist phenomenon in paranormal circles, several cases spring immediately to mind for people interested in the phenomenon. I have tried to find two cases that are not so well known but that give us a good feel for what the poltergeist—whatever that is—might be capable of.

William G. Roll, in his book on the poltergeist, gives an excellent example of the frenetic activity that plagued a family in northeast Kentucky. The activity began in the home of John and Ora Callihan in mid-November 1968. A distinct rumbling noise was heard, and a picture of Jesus fell off the wall, breaking the glass. One might be forgiven for thinking that a passing truck caused the disturbance, but the episodes escalated from that time forward.

Both the coffee table and the kitchen table turned over, seemingly on their own, and a variety of decorative glassware in the home met the same fate as the glass in the picture frame. Roll commented that Mrs. Callihan had two buckets full of broken glass, porcelain, and the remains of four crockery lamps that had been destroyed.

Despite the neighbours' attempts at explanations, no one could really tell the couple what was going on, so, reluctantly, they moved house to a new address in the same community. Roll noted, as well, that the couple's grandson, Roger, came over to help with chores and, when he stayed the night, slept on the floor of his grandparents' room.

Events seemed to quiet down, but a week after moving, Mrs. Callihan thought that she saw an apparition of the deceased owner of the home they had just left. Shortly thereafter, things began to move again. Interestingly, Mrs. Callihan stated that, while this person was "a good man and a good friend", he was also said to be capable of raising "the knocking spirits".

In any event, the Callihans' unusual plight made the front page of the local paper and so came to the attention of Dr. Roll. Roll asked a research associate of his Psychical Research Foundation to check on the case, so on 12 December 1968, John P. Stump came to visit with the Callihans.

Stump observed some of the incidents firsthand as well as collecting accounts from those effected. As is often the case in poltergeist activity, the disturbances were not limited to the immediate family. Mrs. Phyllis Crank, a friend of the Callihans, testified that she had seen some of the movements herself.

The incident that scared Mrs. Crank the most involved the Callihan's grandson, Roger. Mrs. Krank stated that, on 8 December, as she observed Roger walking toward her, a bedstand behind him rose into the air, passed over his head and crashed to the floor in front of him. According to the witness, the object travelled more than ten feet in its flight, and though she had taken the flying crockery in stride, this incident scared her "when I see that force!"

Though it was quiet the night that investigator Stump arrived, that soon changed. The disturbances did seem to centre around twelve-year-old Roger. On one occasion, as Stump observed Roger and his grandparents standing in the kitchen, the investigator saw two bottles and a glass jar containing berries fall into the sink. Stump was unable to find any "natural" mechanism for the falling items.

Later the same day, as John Callihan entered the living room, seeking a place to sit, Stump pointed to a chair. At that precise moment, the chair flipped itself upside down. As before, Roger was sitting nearby, but, again, Stump could see no way that the boy could have caused the event while sitting three feet away in clear view of the investigator.

In another demonstration of the varied powers of the poltergeist, Stump again found himself in the living room, observing young Roger as he sat in a chair, watching television. A harsh cracking sound came from the region of the television set, and Stump stated that he could see that a cloth doily and bowl had fallen down behind the set, while the plastic flowers in the bowl remained on top of the set. As Stump watched, the flowers slid off the top of the television as well and, when the investigator went to look, he saw that the doily, bowl, and flowers were all arranged behind the TV just as they had been while they were on top of the set.

To add to the strangeness, Stump also noted that, at the same time objects were falling behind the television, a clock that had been sitting on the set moved forward and fell to the floor in front of the TV. Stump had no hesitation about contacting Roll and telling him that the case had ongoing activity.

William Roll made his appearance in the story on 14 December. By the time he arrived on scene, Helen, Roger's mother, had been persuaded by members of her church that the activity was caused by demons, something we see all too frequently in paranormal research in the present day. Roll explained his theory of recurring spontaneous psychokinesis and tried to put a scientific spin on the case, but Helen remained unconvinced.

In addition to seeking a more scientific explanation for events, Roll had some serious concerns about young Roger. It seemed that many of the events were occurring in suspiciously close proximity to the boy, and Roll wondered whether the boy might not be helping the "demon" along. When Roger and his family returned to their home from the grandparents', Roll and Stump asked if they could accompany them so that they could get more of their stories.

Roll was soon disabused of the notion that Roger was helping the phenomenon along. At just past midnight on 16 December, in Roger's family home, Roll was walking behind Roger as the boy went into the kitchen. Roger went to the kitchen sink, and as he walked up to the sink, Roll was amazed as the kitchen table "jumped into the air, rotated about forty-five degrees, and came to rest on the backs of the chairs that stood around it, with all four legs off the floor ..."

You can almost hear Roll's puzzlement as he writes:

> At the time of the incident, I was looking directly at Roger and was convinced that he did not push the table. I could discover no other way in which he or anyone else could have caused this event normally. No one else was in the kitchen. The cups and plates, which had been left on the table, crashed to the floor.

Five minutes after this incident, Roll was again present and looking directly at Roger when a coffee table, which weighed more than sixty pounds, flipped over behind the boy. The episode occurred as rapidly as the one with the kitchen table, and though one of Roger's siblings, fourteen-year-old Beverly, was sitting nearby, she was also in Roll's visual range. Given the speed of the incident, it seemed unlikely to Roll or Stump that the girl could have moved the heavy coffee table with such velocity.

Roll asked permission to take pictures of the aftermath of the coffee table incident, and Helen flatly denied them, saying, "No, this has got to stop!" After a further incident where a bottle fell from a dresser, the house seemed to calm down, other than Roger's claims that his pillow was being snatched by an unknown force.

The following morning, Tommy, Roger's father, was on the phone with his parents, the people who had been forced from their home by the disturbances. Tommy commented that the poltergeist seemed to have moved to their house, and, evidently, Helen took umbrage to that statement. She seemed to be convinced that something the investigators had done had caused the "demon" to move to their home, and, in the end, she politely but firmly asked Roll and Stump to leave.

The two left as they were asked, but even after an attempted exorcism by the Callihans' church, the activity continued. Eventually, the family decided to go for a visit to relatives in Ohio, and when they came back, the disturbances did not pick back up again. Dr. Roll was unable to find out if the activity had followed them to Ohio for any period of time.

The Olive Hill case is, in my mind, a very typical poltergeist case with its spontaneous outbreaks of moving objects and shattered glassware. Let's take a look now at a decidedly spooky case with a lot more manifestations happening.

# 5

# THE BLACK MONK OF PONTREFACT

PONTREFACT IS a mid-sized town in West Yorkshire, UK, known as the site of Pontrefact Castle. Richard II was said to have been taken to the castle after being captured by his cousin Henry Bolingbroke in 1399. The deposed monarch was imprisoned in the castle by the newly minted king, Henry IV, and legend has it that Richard starved to death in confinement. In reality, there are three theories about Richard's demise, but history does not tell us exactly what happened to the dethroned monarch, only that he died, apparently at the hands of his captors.

The name of the town derives from Latin, meaning broken bridge. In addition to the castle, Pontrefact was home to a Cluniac priory where local folk tales told the story of a rogue monk who raped a townswoman and paid for his crime by hanging. This tale forms the background of a classic poltergeist case in Colin Wilson's *Poltergeist! A Study in Destructive Haunting*. Unlike the Olive Hill incident, which only lasted a few months, the Pontrefact poltergeist case went on, on and off, for much longer. I will only be able to give the barest of summaries here, but I feel that this case is important since it provides us with a more complete idea of the capabilities of the poltergeist phenomenon.

The activity occurred at 30 East Drive in Pontrefact at the home of Jean and Joe Pritchard. Also involved in the case were the Pritchard's children, Phillip, aged fifteen at the beginning of the haunting, and Diane, age twelve when the activity kicked off. Sarah Scholes, the children's grandmother, was a frequent visitor in the home and a key player in the disturbances.

In August 1966, the family had gone on holiday, and Phillip had decided to stay behind at 30 East Drive with his grandmother. On Thursday of that holiday week, Phillip had gone into the kitchen to get himself some coffee and his grandmother some tea. Mrs. Scholes sat knitting when she noticed a fine white powder settling all around her in the room where she sat. As so often happens in these cases, the grandmother assumed her grandson was up to mischief, but Phillip stated flatly that he had been in the kitchen the whole time.

Mrs. Scholes had noted earlier that the room where she sat seemed cold and that a wind seemed to rattle the windows even though Phillip, who had been sitting outside reading, said that it was calm outside. As Phillip watched the powder, he registered that the mysterious substance was not coming from the ceiling but seemed to "come in" from just above their heads.

Whatever it was, the powder coated everything in the room, and attempts to clean it up were complicated by a new manifestation—puddles of water forming in the kitchen with no apparent cause. Phillip and his grandmother sought help from several neighbours and relatives, one of whom went so far as to turn off the water to the house.

The puddles still formed, and workmen from the local water board could offer no explanation at all. There were no broken pipes, and the drains were all clear.

Despite the weirdness, things eventually settled down in the home only to kick off again later that evening when the button on a tea dispenser was pushed repeatedly by an unseen force, depositing tea and then sugar all over the kitchen counter. Mrs. Scholes yelled at the dispenser to stop, since the button kept pressing in even after the container was empty, and Phillip, who thought he was being accused, said indignantly: "I can't—it's doing it on its own!"

After the events in the kitchen, the poltergeist settled into a favourite poltergeist game: hide-and-seek. The occupants of the house would hear a crash and run to one part of the house. They would find some damage, such as a plant torn from a pot, only to hear another crash, this time in the kitchen. When they arrived in the kitchen, they would find the cupboards vibrating as though someone or something was trying to get out.

Marie Kelly, another of Mrs. Scholes' children, lived across the street and witnessed the vibrating cupboards. As before, the disturbance calmed down, tea was had, and the house's occupants retired for the night—or tried to. When Mrs. Scholes came in to wish Phillip good night, he watched over her shoulder as a cupboard in the corner of the room staggered about "like a drunken man". The two had endured enough. They abandoned the house to sleep at the Kellys' that night.

After some further incidents, the activity settled down for almost two years. Phillip departed school and went to work in the family's pet shop, and Diane moved into her teenage years. Mrs. Scholes, now in her early seventies, spent most weekends with the family, and, it seems, she never forgot the strangeness of the August Bank Holiday two years previously. As that holiday approached again, she commented on the earlier episodes only to be actively discouraged by the family's father, Joe.

It may be that Mrs. Scholes was having a presentiment of things to come, or it may be that, like other experiencers of poltergeist phenomena, she was acutely aware when the activity was about to happen. As Mrs. Scholes and Jean Pritchard were taking tea, they both heard a sound in the hallway.

Jean found the counterpane (an English term for a bedspread) from her bed at the foot of the stairs. No one had been in the hall, and the item had not been there ten minutes before when she came into the kitchen. The woman put the counterpane back in its proper place and returned to the task that had been occupying her attention before her tea break—redecorating Diane's bedroom upstairs.

A loud crash sounded, and, upon investigation, Mrs. Pritchard found another counterpane, this one from Phillip's room, lying in the hallway. The crash had come from several plants being tipped over onto the carpet.

Mrs. Scholes, of course, was quite upset, stating flatly that the disturbances were beginning again. She decided to return home, but that evening, Mrs. Pritchard was having trouble going to sleep. She decided to have a look at the room she was redecorating.

For whatever reason, checking on her handiwork seemed to have triggered whatever force was haunting the house. As Mrs. Pritchard watched, a paintbrush flew by her head, a paste bucket levitated, a strip of wallpaper stood up and began to writhe like a snake, and the carpet sweeper began to move around the room as though some invisible person was wielding it as a club.

Mrs. Pritchard's fear-filled vocalizations raised the rest of the house, and the activity took off in earnest. Objects began to fly around at random, and Diane was struck by a hairbrush. There was some concern for the teen since the brush seemed to be travelling at a clip that should have knocked her down. Amazingly, the girl told her parents that the object had just tapped her.

In addition to the flying household objects, Phillip watched as a pelmet, a narrow border of wood used to conceal curtain rods and fittings, was ripped from the wall and thrown out the window. The young man actually heard the object hit the path below. Not only had the pelmet flown away of its own accord, but it had also done so despite being bolted to the wall with two-inch screws.

The activity seemed to centre itself in Diane's bedroom, and when he realized this, Diane's father angrily slammed the door to the room and forbad Diane from opening it. The family could hear banging and slamming from inside the room both before and after the door was closed.

That night seemed to be the kick-off of nine months of activity. Wilson tells us that life with the "ghost" (or whatever it was) seemed to settle into a sort of routine. The activity usually began around bedtime with a series of knocks and would then proceed to objects flying around rooms and the lights going on and off. Often lights would go out, and when someone looked at the switch box under the stairs, the switches would be off. Mr. Pritchard tried to stop this by taping the switches in the on position but, when the lights went off again, returned to find the switches turned to the off position and the tape nowhere to be seen.

The Pritchards turned to their church for assistance, and when the local vicar came over to discuss the possibility of an exorcism, nothing happened in the home ... at first. As the priest was preparing to go, a candlestick fell off the mantel. The skeptical clergyman credited subsidence until another candlestick floated up off the mantel, moved across the room and then fell to the floor.

As the priest was absorbing this incident, a resounding noise sounded from the kitchen. Everyone rushed into the room to find every single piece of dishware from a cabinet on the floor. Astonishingly, despite the ruckus, nothing was broken except the clergyman's faith in a natural explanation for the event.

That same night, as if to show that it meant no real harm, Mr. Nobody, as the family had christened their "ghost", pinned Diane to the stairs with a set of heavy furniture that should have crushed her. Interestingly, the objects that held her in place, a sewing machine and hall stand, could not be moved until she stopped panicking.

Wilson noted that, while the force in the home was always noisy, it was also seen to evince several other characteristics. It could be quite inventive, as with the mysteriously appearing white dust in the first days of the case, or it could be flat-out destructive, as when a grandfather clock was tossed from its place and seemed to explode like a bomb. The energy could even be almost seductive. It sometimes announced its presence with a sweet smell, a counterpoint to the foul odour seen in some cases.

What is clear is that whatever the "ghost" was, it was an intelligent force. When Maude Peerce, Mrs. Pritchard's sister, came to visit, she was convinced that the poltergeist was a big joke that the family was playing on everyone. Mrs. Peerce was soon disabused of this notion. As she sat in the kitchen with her sister, the lights went out again. A fire was lit in the kitchen so that all could see as the refrigerator opened, the milk slid out and then proceeded to pour itself over Mrs. Peerce's head.

The spluttering aunt promptly accused the children of mischief, but Mrs. Pritchard would have none of that, stating firmly that the children were standing next to her while their aunt got an impromptu milk shower. If Mrs. Peerce was so convinced that the whole thing was a prank, Mrs. Pritchard offered, then she was welcome to stay the night and see for herself.

The aunt accepted the challenge and removed her hat and coat but could not find one of her gloves. The family moved into the living room, and, again, the lights went off. There was a violent banging noise, and when Mrs. Pritchard had again gone to the switch box below the stairs and turned the electricity back on, the house was in disarray. The chairs had been turned upside down, the electric fireplace had been pulled out of its spot, and the contents of the refrigerator, including a string of sausages, sat on the floor around them.

Having had enough for the evening, the poltergeist seemed to retire and so did the family, including Mrs. Peerce. The aunt eventually found her missing glove the next day—floating in mid-air as though a hand were fisted inside it. Mrs. Peerce, a devout Christian, began to sing a hymn, and the glove mockingly directed the tune for her. The aunt departed the house and declared that she would not return for twenty thousand pounds (remember, this case takes place in the UK).

The episodes continued with the poltergeist evincing great inventiveness in its pranks. The force seemed to be capable of making items disappear from one place and appear in another. Mrs. Pritchard had a problem with eggs disappearing from the refrigerator and then floating into a room only to explode as "beautiful smelling bombs". The woman placed the eggs under a crate and sat on the crate only to have eggs continue to appear and explode. When she checked the eggs under the crate, it was clear that the poltergeist had been able to access them anyway.

The poltergeist did not appreciate any attempts to get rid of it. When Vic Kelly, Marie Kelly's husband, tried to move the "ghost" along with holy water and prayers, as per his priest, the poltergeist responded with strong anti-Christian sentiment, throwing Diane out of bed several times that night and sticking a crucifix to her back later the next day. On Easter morning, the family returned from church to find that the mischievous force had spray-painted upside-down crosses on the walls.

As the poltergeist case moved toward its denouement, it was evident that the "ghost" was becoming more powerful. The banging noises it made were deafening, and it added barnyard noises to its repertoire of sounds in addition to "stertorous breathing". Even more frightening, both Joe and Jean Pritchard as well as their next-door neighbour, Mrs. May, saw the apparition that gave the case its name—a black figure than seemed to be wearing a hooded monk's habit.

The situation came to a head when Diane went into the kitchen to make coffee and the lights went out. The family heard the teenager scream and rushed to find her being dragged up the stairs, her cardigan stretched in front of her as though something had hold of it. It was also apparent that some force had the girl by the throat. Whereas the poltergeist had refrained from harming Diane before, it did not hold back this time, and the family had to wrestle the young woman away from the force.

Terribly shaken, Diane was given some brandy to calm her, and both Mrs. Pritchard and Phillip noted the angry red finger marks on the teen's throat.

This scary incident was followed shortly by one in which Mrs. Pritchard came downstairs only to find the carpet in the hall completely soaked with water. As she was studying the mess, she saw "huge footprints'" forming on the sodden surface.

While activity and sightings of the poltergeist continued for a while after these events, the disturbances began to taper off after the Pritchards decided to try an old folk remedy for banishing spirits. They hung dried garlic all over the house, and it seemed to have the desired effect. Whether this was due to the apotropaic effects of garlic or the Pritchards' belief in the remedy, I will leave up to the reader to decide.

Colin Wilson sums up this case by saying, "I can find nothing like him [speaking of the poltergeist] in the annals of this type of haunting. The sounds, the smells, the animal noises, the heavy breathing, the bites on a sandwich, and, finally, the appearance, make him almost unique."

# 6

## KNOCKS, RAPS, AND CLACKS

NOW THAT WE have had a chance to outline what a class B encounter and a poltergeist case are, I want to begin to look at some of the specific similarities between the two.

Researcher Ken Gerhard, in *The Essential Guide to Bigfoot*, has this to say about the hallmark sound associated with Sasquatch in the forest—the wood knock:

---

A potential form of nonverbal communication that has been associated with Bigfoot for decades involves loud, percussive knocking noises that emanate in the forest, typically referred to as "tree knocks" or "wood knocks." Many researchers associate these sounds with Sasquatches, though I have only been able to locate a single account describing one of the creatures actually banging on a tree with a piece of wood in order to produce a knock (this allegedly was observed by a Colorado elk hunter during the summer of 2009). Eyewitness Elmer Frombach of Washington State claimed that he observed one of the creatures banging large rocks together during his 1994 encounter. He had initially become aware of the sound echoing through the woods before confronting the animal.

---

The United States is not the only place where witnesses have encountered this strange phenomenon. A good example of a class B wood-knocking incident happened to a retired mail carrier along Highway 66 in Alberta, Canada. In BFRO report #59610, the witness tells us that he was setting up his camera equipment at about 2145 hours when the incident occurred. The retiree was working on developing his photography as a side business and wanted to get some pictures of the sunset that evening.

As he was sitting in his car, "waiting for the right amount of sunlight", he heard a wood knock but did not think anything of it. A second knock sounded, and the witness went to the back of his car and retrieved a baseball bat, responding to the knock with one of his own. He stated that he did not really think he would get a response, but about two minutes later, another knock sounded at a range the witness estimated as about one kilometre.

The witness then moved to a different tree and responded, and when the response came this time, the retiree estimated that it came from no more than three hundred metres away. At this point, the witness was not sure what was responding to his knocks, but he got a camera out to see if he might get a picture of whatever it was.

The witness waited for a short time, then picked up the bat and knocked again. The previous sounds had come from north of the highway, but almost immediately after he knocked, the witness heard a "scream-howl" from the south side of the highway, followed by a knock, again from the north.

After these two sounds, the incident came to a close.

The reader may recall from BFRO report #16944, cited in the beginning of this text, the witness statement of a hunter who had a hair-raising (literally) encounter with something in the forests of Ontario near the border to the massive Algonquin Provincial Park. I won't repeat the whole story again, but it is notable that, in addition to the silence that descended during the encounter, the feeling of being watched and the sourceless fear that seemed to raise the hair on the back of his neck, the witness also reported wood knocks.

The sequence began with four knocks, stopped for thirty seconds or so, and continued with a further four or five knocks. The witness, who described himself as a very large person, stated emphatically that there was no way that he "could ... have hit two pieces of wood together that loud".

The knocking went on for about ten minutes and seemed to be getting closer to the witness, who decided to follow his first instinct, when the strangeness began, and vacated the area. He returned to the camper where he and his party met up. The others in the hunting group had heard the sounds, but they were so scattered that the knocking was distant to them. No one in the party could explain the sounds.

Wood or trees are not the only things that are struck in these incidents. Another class B episode occurred in March 2006 near Chilliwack, British Columbia. In BFRO report #14020, the witness and a hiking partner had broken camp after what the witness describes as a "chilly night's stay at Lindeman Lake in the Chilliwack River Valley". The two hikers had moved about fifteen minutes down the trail with the witness in the lead, some distance ahead of the hiking partner. The witness heard a "banging noise" coming from the trees ahead, and when the partner caught up, the witness asked if he had heard the sound.

The hiking partner stated that he thought the witness had made the sound. The witness had not made the sounds and said so, and the two listened as more "banging sounds" continued. The witness reported that at this point the noises sounded like two rocks banging together. He or she does not state whether the initial knocks were on wood or also sounded like stones clacking together.

As the duo continued to listen, they realized that the sounds were coming from two different locations approximately seventy to one hundred feet into the tree line. As both witnesses were certified search and rescue technicians, they were concerned that the clacks might be a distress call. The witness listened intently for a pattern and discerned that the clacks came in series of no more than six.

When the witness' hiking partner struck two stones together several times, the sounds abruptly ceased and did not resume. The two continued their hike out but stopped several times in order to listen for further sounds.

In another rock-knocking report, this one in BFRO report #12100, another pair of hikers were finishing up a long and, apparently, soggy seven-day journey bushwhacking through the Boise Valley, north of Pitt Lake in British Columbia. The couple stopped along their way and made a small fire in order to warm up and dry their clothes.

As the couple sat, enjoying the warmth, something strange occurred:

> After about a half hour there, we heard a strange noise coming from the forest on the south side of the road. The sound could be described as two rocks being struck together. This in itself was not so strange, but the sound repeated itself at regular intervals of 5 seconds or so, on and off, for a good ten minutes. Immediately after this started, our dogs put their tails between their legs—showing absolutely NO desire to find out what was making the sound. This was perhaps even stranger than the noises.

Both hikers stood and called into the trees, thinking that a person must be about, but they got no response. In addition, the couple experienced the same raising of the hair on the back of their necks that we saw in the Northern Ontario witness. The male witness was considering going to see what the source of the sounds was, but his female companion, who had experienced a possible Sasquatch sighting sometime before this incident, was insistent that they depart the area.

The hikers doused their fire and got underway "at a fast walk". Once the two had gotten a few minutes down the trail, the sounds, which they could still hear clearly, stopped completely.

It seems clear that, whatever it is people are encountering in the forest, it has a distinct liking for wood knocking and the related stone clacking. Interestingly, there are researchers, such as the Olympic Project team, who feel that the creatures might be drumming. A look at the Olympic Project website yields a page called Friday Night drumming that has recordings, taken in the wilds of Washington, that do indeed sound like drumming. This idea has direct tie-ins to the poltergeist phenomenon, especially to a case called the Phantom Drummer of Tedworth, in which one of the main manifestations of the phenomenon was the sounding of an actual drum, which drove the victim family to distraction.

Dr. Jeff Meldrum, in his excellent *Sasquatch: Legend meets Science,* notes that great apes use wood knocking as a means of communication. According to the doctor, chimpanzees split into groups to forage during the day and have been observed doing wood knocks to maintain contact with other groups and, perhaps, relay their position to others of their clan. Chimps have also been observed to "drum" on trees in times of excitement.

Gorillas use a similar method of communication when they forage, slapping the ground to relay their position to the others of their group. A female silverback has been observed to clap her hands together to attract the attention of a male nearby, and in addition, the slapping of trees, the ground and even the chest is used as an intimidation display.

So the wood-knocking behaviour is certainly within the purview of an undiscovered primate, but we must also note that wood knocking is a classic sign of another strange phenomenon: the poltergeist.

Those who are familiar with the history of the Spiritualist movement in the United States will know that the Fox sisters, who kicked off this movement through their communication with the supposed spirit of a murdered peddler, discovered that they could "speak" with the spirit using a simple code. When the spirit wanted to reply "yes", it would rap a table once. When it wanted to respond "no", the spirit would rap twice. While the

Fox sisters later confessed that their communication was all a hoax, they recanted this confession, so we can never be certain how much of their experience was real and how much was produced in some way to satisfy the hordes of people who looked to them.

The raps described by the Fox sisters and others who took part in nineteenth-century seances are not the only evidence of "noisy spirits" manifesting through rapping and banging.

In his investigations of the Thornton Heath poltergeist case in the 1930s, Nandor Fodor described something that he called the "phantom hammer". In that day when psychical research was moving out from under the wings of Spiritualism and looking to modern science and psychology for experimental rigour, Fodor had witnessed the activity in his subject's home. The researcher had decided to bring the focus of the activity into the headquarters of the International Institute for Psychical Research, where he worked, to perform spiritualist sessions. The working theory at the time was that the focus of poltergeist events must be a spiritual medium. Fodor describes the phantom hammer incident as he and the other members of the Institute present were testing the subject for psychokinesis:

---

Next, Mrs. Forbes [the subject] was asked to sit in the opening of the cabinet on a wooden chair. The curtain was drawn to her shoulders. In a cabinet on a folding table there were five tumblers, one holding a rattle, another a spent flashlight bulb. She had a saucer and a teacup in her hands.

Presently we were introduced to the phenomenon of the phantom hammer ... the secretary came in and the disturbance thus created made most of us turn toward the door. At this moment of diversion there was [a] loud PING, and the cup and saucer flew out of Mrs. Forbes' hands ...

Three witnesses saw the saucer in the air broken, one saw it in the process of breaking after it left Mrs. Forbes' hand. Subsequently, not the strongest of us was able to break a saucer of that thickness in his hands, nor was it possible to produce the sound on the saucer while it was being held.

---

While Fodor is not describing a table rap or other sort of wood knock, it is interesting to note that the poltergeist seems capable of generating interesting sounds that are difficult to duplicate.

Hans Holzer, in his epic work *Ghosts: True Encounters with the World Beyond*, describes the case of the Leuthold farm poltergeist in Switzerland, 1960. The farm was plagued by things moving about and items disappearing and reappearing. The farmer related the following example of the poltergeist's mischief:

---

My wife and I were inside the house. Suddenly, there was a knock at the door which sounded as if it was made by a hard object. My wife was in the kitchen. She left her work and went to look outside. There was no one outside. Shortly after, there was another knock. The maid was downstairs in her room and she didn't see anyone either. My wife went back to her work. Soon there was a third set of knocks. This time, she was

alerted and kept close to the door. As soon as she heard
the knocking, she jumped outside.

---

Interestingly, when the wife opened the door, she observed a
piece of wood dropping to the ground about a foot from the
door. In other words, the poltergeist had been using wood to
strike the wooden door and produce a sound, just as Sasquatch
are theorized to do in class B encounters.

Janet and Colin Bord, in *Modern Mysteries of the World,* tell of
a poltergeist whose knocking was so loud that it could be heard
from across the road from the house where the disturbance was
occurring—a distance of over sixty yards. This incident
occurred in Fougères-sur-Bièvre, France, in December 1913,
and, as with Sasquatch-related reports, the energy involved
showed some intelligence, responding to a certain number of
raps by witnesses with the same number of raps.

In his on-scene description of the Enfield poltergeist case, *This
House is Haunted,* Guy Playfair describes similar knocking
behaviour. In the first manifestation of the event, the poltergeist
made its presence known by making four strong raps on the wall
of the home. When the frightened family went to their neighbours, the neighbours also heard the knocks. One of the neighbours moved around the house, and the knocks seemed to follow
him. He was certain that kids in the area had to be having them
on and went into the alley to check. No children were in
evidence, but the knocking continued.

The constables were summoned (the case takes place in the
UK), and they, too, heard the knocks, four at a time, and were
unable to find a cause despite searching the area thoroughly.
Interestingly, the witnesses noted that the knocks had a "curious

hollow sound" to them, as if someone were in the wall trying to get out.

Playfair, in the summation to his book, notes that rapping sounds are a commonality of many of the poltergeist cases he had researched or personally investigated. He says:

> ... rapping and thumping on the floor seems to be a way that poltergeists draw attention. This they certainly succeed in doing in my experience, but I have not yet found a way of discovering what it is that the attention is supposed to be attracted to.

I think that this sentiment might be repeated by those who investigate the Sasquatch phenomenon. It is clear that something in the woods is making these rapping and banging sounds or clacking stones together, but the purpose is never clear. Those who believe Sasquatch is an unknown great ape are content to believe that this is simply the behaviour of said ape and point to chimpanzees and gorillas as exemplars.

I am not so sure, and as we progress through the many areas of the class B incidents and compare them with poltergeist phenomena, we will make a good case for something far stranger than a hidden ape or hominid in the forests of North America.

# 7

# STONE THROWING

ANOTHER OF THE very common behaviours delineated in class B incidents is stone throwing. We saw that this was the behaviour that caused so much excitement in the "Sasquatch Attacks" episode of *MonsterQuest*, and it is an action that we see over and over in the annals of Sasquatch witness reports. More than one witness has said that bears and other forest animals do not throw stones, and noted crypto-zoologist Ken Gerhard in his book *The Essential Guide to Bigfoot*, comments that "... unless there is a secret society of deep-woods catapult enthusiasts, this phenomenon does seem quite inexplicable."

In BFRO report #51949, two ghost hunters in Nova Scotia had a class B incident while searching for the ghost supposedly seen at Uniacke Estate Museum Park. The two witnesses had travelled to a spot near Uniacke Lake where the ghost had reportedly been seen. They approached to within twenty yards of the bench where the apparition had been spotted when a "heavy rock flew in front of [them] into the lake and [they] heard it hit the rocks under the water". The witness turned on his flashlight but was unable to see anyone who could have thrown the rock.

The distance from the copse of trees where the stone originated and the lake was about fifteen meters (about forty-nine feet).

It seems, from this description, that the object must have been thrown with considerable force, and the incident certainly impressed the witnesses, who departed immediately and had not been back to the site after dark at the time of the report. This case is also an interesting example of the silo effect in para-normal research. The two witnesses were actually out looking for ghosts, but when a rock soars out of the forest near them, at least one of the witnesses instantly defaults to Sasquatch. We'll see why that is fallacious thinking as we proceed through this chapter and, eventually, the entire book.

Another stone-throwing incident occurred near the unincorpo-rated town of Shebandowan in west central Ontario. BFRO report #23490 tells the story of a witness who was visiting the family cottage during the summer of 2005. The witness was paddling Lake Shebandowan with his older brother when the two heard a commotion in the brush onshore. Trees swayed back and forth as the disturbance got closer, and the paddlers decided to retreat to their side of the lake, returning to the cabin with considerable haste.

It seemed to the brothers that they might have been witness to a large moose rambling through the underbrush, and it is entirely possible that this was the source of the initial encounter; however, later events proved far stranger. Around midnight, the two brothers and a couple of companions boarded a power boat and puttered back across the lake to the site of their earlier encounter. They cut the engine "20 or so feet from shore" and sat quietly, perhaps trying to discern what they had experienced earlier.

As the experiencers later reported to BFRO field investigator Todd Prescott, a few minutes after they stopped their craft "a small object splashed into the water close to the boat". About twenty seconds later, another object struck the water. The witnesses are not noted to have responded, so about a minute after the initial contact, a larger, heavier object landed very close to the boat.

The boat engine was quickly restarted, and once again, the witness and his companions made a quick retreat to the cabin. No other sounds were heard in this encounter, and the witnesses were careful to note that there were no trees over-hanging the lake in that area so the objects/stones could not have fallen into the lake from a tree.

The area where the witnesses had their encounter is a lake that investigator Prescott states is thirty miles long by two miles wide and surrounded by "dense, mixed forest". It made no sense to any of the witnesses that any human would go to through the trouble of pushing their way through the thick foliage for an opportunity to throw rocks at a passing boat in the middle of the night.

It seems that our "catapult enthusiasts" have a wide range since we also have reports of rock throwing from the Pacific side of Canada, specifically Vancouver Island. In BFRO report #15571, the witnesses, a husband and wife with their son, had driven up a logging road and then proceeded to go deeper into the bush until they camped at the mouth of Forbush Lake. They were well over an hour from the logging road, which was only accessible during daylight hours due to its ruggedness.

At about 0500 hours, the son awoke and told his parents that he had heard something crossing the river that fed into the lake. Being an experienced hiker and camper, the father did not think much of this information until he heard what sounded like rocks being thrown into the water. The father exited the tent to investigate and heard what seemed to be another stone hitting the water.

The witness got his family up and into the small boat they had with them, then rowed them out into the lake. As he said in his report, he "didn't know what else to do". As the family floated in the dark about forty feet from the shore, the father scanned the darkness with a flashlight. He reported seeing what could have been red eye shine, but, otherwise, there seemed to be nothing in the area.

Nevertheless, the family remained in their boat until the sun came up and did not venture back to shore until it was full light. The incident scared their son so badly that the group packed up and left. The father, who filed the report, states clearly that there is no other way to get to the site but hiking or paddling and that there was no one else in the area, Additionally, there were no other cars in the area when they got back to their truck.

In another incident in British Columbia, a couple and their child were camping in their motor home on the shore of Batnuni Lake. BFRO report #6579 gives us the details.

The husband had gone into the motor home to put the couple's five-year-old to bed, and at the child's request, the father had lain down with the little one until she went to sleep. In the meantime, the wife was sitting outside with the family dogs, enjoying some quiet time and the warmth of a blazing fire on that August evening.

As so often happens, the first sign that something was amiss occurred when the dogs, two Rottweilers and a pug, began to bark and growl in the direction of the lake. The female witness had her back to the lake and thought nothing of the animals' disturbance. Instead, she tried to quiet the dogs so that they would not wake sleeping children.

Abruptly, there was a "huge splash" in the lake, which set the dogs off again and caused the wife to reprimand what she thought was her husband playing a practical joke. The wife, still thinking her husband was having her on, got progressively angrier as two more rocks fell into the water near her. As the female witness stated, "there is no mistaking the sound of big boulders going over the bank into the water ... that hollow kerploosh sound". The dogs were no longer barking but were standing with their hackles raised, growling.

Having had quite enough of this seeming prank, the wife went back into the RV to get a flashlight so that she could flush out her husband. Anger turned to tears of fear when the woman discovered her husband in the motor home instead of out pushing rocks into the lake. She quickly informed her husband of the disturbance, and the male witness went to investigate.

He, too, heard the sound of rocks falling into the water. After two more loud splashes, the couple got up the nerve to go investigate, and the sounds stopped when they turned a flashlight on to have a look around. Interestingly, none of the dogs would exit the RV with the couple.

The witnesses were veteran campers who had heard beavers slap and seen and heard various large animals in the water. In their experience, nothing came close to the sounds they heard that night. As the reporting party puts it, "whatever was throwing the big boulders into the lake from that high up and to get them that far out into the lake had to be big and very very strong".

The item that all these incidents have in common is that no one actually saw the rock thrower. As I noted in *Sasquatch Canada,* even with the aid of modern technology, these rock throwers remain consistently hard to catch. In the "Sasquatch Attacks" episode of *MonsterQuest*, mentioned above, the searchers had the advantage of infrared and night-vision cameras when looking for their stone thrower and were still unable to catch the culprit.

Dr. Meldrum is of the opinion that stone throwing is yet another sign that Sasquatch is a great ape or related species. In *Sasquatch: Legend Meets Science*, the good doctor notes that rock throwing is a common sign of aggression amongst chimpanzees. I concur that the behaviour often seems to denote aggression and perhaps even some concern for territorial integrity, but I don't think this automatically points us to the ape family alone.

If, once again, we step outside the bounds of "conventional" Sasquatch research and look to the history of the poltergeist phenomenon, we see that there is a force that cannot be perceived by human eyes that is quite happy to throw stones and, indeed, is noted for it.

Many people are of the mistaken impression that all the early ghost hunters were doughty men of science trying to explore the "Other Side", but women played a strong role in the early annals of paranormal investigation as well. Catherine Crowe, in her seminal work *The Night-Side of Nature; Or, Ghosts and Ghost-Seers,* cites a couple of historical examples of poltergeist activity that included stone throwing.

In one example from the year 1670, Crowe tells us of an episode at Keppock, near Glasgow, Scotland, in which "stones were thrown which hit nobody, but the annoyance only continued eight days". Additionally, at around the same period, Crowe tells of a disturbance that happened around the house of one Gilbert Cambell:

Here, as elsewhere, stones were thrown; but, as in most similar instances I meet with, no human being was damaged—the license of these spirits, or goblins, or whatever they be, seeming to extend no further than worrying and tormenting their victims. In this case, however, the spirit spoke to them, though he was never seen. The annoyance commenced in November, of the year 1654, I think, and continued till April, when there was some intermission till July, when it recommenced. The loss of the family from the things destroyed was ruining; for their household goods and chattels were rendered useless, their food was polluted and spoiled, and their very clothes cut to pieces while on their backs, by invisible hands; and it was in vain that all the ministers about the country assembled to exorcise this troublesome spirit, for whoever was there the thing continued exactly the same.

I think it is important to note that, not only did this force throw stones, but it also vocalized, something we will discuss at some length later in the book, and caused general mayhem around the home, something that our theoretical forest poltergeist seems capable of as well when we consider some of the other "signs" of Sasquatch presence in an area.

We do not have to go back to 1670 to see stone-throwing poltergeists, however.

Colin Wilson, in his book on poltergeists, comments on a 1906 case in Sumatra where the hapless householder, a Mr. Grottendieck, was awakened by a shower of stones that seemed to be falling from the sky ... except that they were penetrating the roof of his "makeshift house". When the man angrily fired a rifle into the air, the storm of stones only intensified—a behaviour that we see in Sasquatch-related cases, where the firing of a weapon only results in larger stones being thrown.

Interestingly, when Mr. Grottendieck tried to grab one of the stones from mid-air, the object seemed to actively avoid his attempt to catch it. As we noted in earlier poltergeist cases, it is not uncommon and, indeed, expected, for objects propelled by the poltergeist force to halt in mid-air or make ninety-degree course variations while in flight. One wonders what might happen if a witness attempted to catch one of the rocks thrown in a class B episode.

In his fascinating book on the 1977 Enfield poltergeist case, Guy Lyon Playfair speaks of incidents where people in the house observed marbles and Legos (there were no stones in the house, of course) flying through the air.

---

Somebody, or something was flinging marbles and bits of Jimmy's Lego toy bricks around, or rather shooting them *as if from a catapult* [emphasis from author]. They would just zoom out of thin air and bounce off the walls, or drop straight to the floor as if they had come straight through the ceiling ...

---

A photographer for the *Daily Mirror* newspaper, Graham Morris, was introduced to the phenomenon in a serious manner.

As he was attempting to take a photo of some of the activity happening, the photographer caught movement out of the corner of his eye and was struck just above his right eye by what appeared to be a Lego brick. When Playfair was introduced to the photographer a week later, the man still had a sizeable bruise in the place where the object had impacted.

Playfair points out about this incident that it was "quite obvious that nobody in the room had thrown the Lego ... the only two people facing the camera as the brick flew across the room" either had their hands in their pockets or had their arms folded as Morris clicked the shot that preceded his injury. Additionally, Lego bricks, while painful to walk on, do not have a lot of mass. Throwing a Lego should not have resulted in an injury that lasted for a week or more.

Playfair lists some commonalities of the poltergeist experience later in *This House is Haunted*, and number one on his list is stone throwing. The author says:

> This is often the first stage. When it occurs at all on a case, it tends to occur before any other kind of phenomenon. Stones or bricks bombard the roof to the victim's house, sometimes appearing inside the house even when doors and windows are closed—as they tend to be when this sort of thing starts to happen!

Playfair does not just mention the stone-throwing incidents in *This House is Haunted*. In another book, *The Indefinite Boundary*, Playfair tells the story of Maria Jose Ferreira of Jabuticabal, Brazil. This unfortunate child was eventually driven to suicide by the poltergeist that plagued her. The phenomenon started in December of 1965 when Ferreira's family began to notice brick pieces falling in the house, seemingly from nowhere. There were no bricks in the house, but there was a pile of the objects outside the house.

After a failed Catholic exorcism, the family turned to a Spiritist neighbour, a dentist named Joao Volpe. Volpe quickly discerned that the focus of the activity was eleven-year-old Maria Jose and offered to take her into his home to see if anything could be done to stop the phenomenon.

---

For a few days all was quiet, but then stones began to fly around the Volpe home whenever Maria Jose was around. The bombardment became so intense that Volpe was finally able to count a total of 312 stones of all shapes and sizes, one weighing no less than 3.7 kilos [a little over eight pounds] ...

---

This incident seems to put even the Ape Canyon story of Sasquatch pelting a cabin with stones to shame.

I do not dispute the evidence for Sasquatch. The reader will hear me say this again and again throughout these pages, in interviews and in my previous book. It seems evident to me that the many eyewitnesses to this creature are seeing something. What that something is, I and all other investigators can only conjecture.

What we cannot do is make assumptions, and thus my attempt, in these pages, to present an alternate theory or theories for what may be making disturbances in the forest. I am quite happy to believe that a certain number of these cases are, indeed, Sasquatch giving humans something to think about besides themselves. But I also feel that there is far more going on out in the forest.

We have seen now that two of the well-known signs that make investigators assume a Sasquatch is nearby are actually common in poltergeist cases. Let's look now at another of the seemingly common signs of Sasquatch presence—tree structures and nests.

# 8
## REARRANGING THE ENVIRONMENT

SASQUATCH EXIST. What they are, exactly, we do not know, but it is plain that the creature, which is well known to the Native people of North America, is out there. As I noted in *Sasquatch Canada,* however, even the indigenous people don't have a set view of what Sasquatch is. Some see the creature as just another animal in the woods, while others take a far more spiritual view of the Hairy One.

In many ways, these differences are reflected in the many theories that surround the Sasquatch in researcher culture. Those who want to show that Sasquatch is simply an unknown ape are fond of pointing to the locations, known for Sasquatch sightings, where mysterious tree structures are found and where large nests can be seen.

According to Dr. Meldrum, such behaviour is in line with the behaviour of the great apes. Birute Gablikas, in her first encounter with an orangutan, observed the great ape pushing over a tree (presumably as an intimidation display). It is easy to imagine a Sasquatch, with its enormous size, pushing over trees and even manipulating them to create some of the intricate tree structures described by researchers.

Great apes have not been described making the kinds of intricate structures observed by Sasquatch field researchers, but I am willing to make the assumption that Sasquatch are next-level intelligent and may have some arcane purpose for building these structures. Researchers have theorized that the bent trees could serve as everything from territorial markers to orienteering aids to hunting blinds. Like so many things in the Sasquatch world, the true purpose of the observed structures is a mystery.

In addition, great apes are certainly known to create sleeping nests of foliage, grass, ferns, leafy vegetation, and boughs. Sasquatch researchers have documented similar, huge, nest-like structures in areas where Sasquatch sightings are common. These researchers believe that their erstwhile subjects may sleep in the open in a position similar to that adopted by gorillas and use these nests, as the great apes seem to, to enhance their comfort and, perhaps, to provide some camouflage.

So let's look briefly at tree structures first.

Researcher Richard L Soule, on the Nox Gigas Study website, outlines several different types of structures that he observed in his investigations in Nebraska. He noted arches, where saplings had seemingly been pulled down to the ground to make an arched structure, as well, X structures where two trees are placed in an X shape, sometimes suspended above the ground. Soule also observed piles of sticks that seemed to have been deliberately placed (Soule theorized that these were the work of juvenile Sasquatch) and what he calls tipi structures, which resemble to frame for the Native dwelling of the same name. In addition to all these finds, Soule also catalogs structures that he calls lean-tos, blinds/shelters, asterisks, and a number of others.

In *The Essential Guide to Bigfoot,* author Ken Gerhard tells us that one of the most impressive tree structures he has encountered in his research was "a twenty-foot tree at least a foot in diameter that had been laid into the fork of another tree at a perfect ninety-degree angle, so that it rocked up and down like a seesaw when touched on either end". Gerhard also notes one set of structures that he witnessed that gave some support to the theory that the structures are created for navigational purposes:

Once, while investigating so-called "Skunk Ape" evidence in Florida's Green Swamp, I found several stick structures in a line, spaced about thirty yards apart. I hiked in the direction that they seemed to all be pointing in and ended up at a tiny pond that was well obscured by surrounding brush. It was almost as if the structures were serving as a road map to the hidden water source.

The Sasquatch Investigations of the Rockies website contains an entire page of pictures of a "tree structure complex" found by the site founder, Michael Johnson. Some of the pics seem to show tree falls that could have happened naturally, but the sheer density of these structures in the given area seems to argue for something more than natural causes. Some of these "markers" though really do seem to have been created by an intelligence. In some of the photos, it is apparent that the trees have not just been placed but have been bent into shapes to form a sort of design. If these structures are being created by humans, for some unknown reason, then they are being accomplished with great stealth and heavy tools.

Just as ubiquitous in Sasquatch research as the tree structures are the numerous researchers who mention finding what they believe are nesting sites.

BFRO report #26821 tells the story of a father and his two sons who were out looking for signs of Sasquatch in the mountainous forest near Falkland, British Columbia. During the course of their investigative trip, they found several possible nests, some of which seem to have been combined with stick structures that overlay the site.

> But the coolest thing that day was we ran into 9-10 possible nests. I was off the road right by our van and the others were up on the other side of the hill. (I have pics from my phone if you would like to see them.) We climbed the hill and saw more farther up. At least they looked like shelters that were built by trees pushed over and bent in an arch with other sticks laid in different positions around the shelter. Some were laid straight and next to each other while others were on top of each other.

The late and sorely missed researcher Linda Godfrey mentions a nest site in conjunction with a Sasquatch report that she investigated. In her article entitled "Kettles, Cows and Sasquatch: Bigfoot in Southern Wisconsin" found in volume one of the *Wood Knocks* journal, Godfrey relates the 1993 case of a young man who disturbed a Sasquatch in the barn on his family property. Fortunately, this particular Sasquatch was not of the more aggressive type and departed after being discovered. When the witness reported the sighting to his parents, they called the local sheriff's department.

Investigating deputies found "a large, nest-like circular area tramped down in the grass outside the barn". Even more interesting, the deputy commented that there had been other Sasquatch reports from a nearby town. One wonders if Wisconsin public servants aren't more forthcoming than others; it was a folder marked "werewolf" that Godfrey found in the files of her local animal control officer that set her on the path of the legendary Manwolf or Dogman.

Ken Gerhard, in his afore-mentioned Sasquatch book, notes possible nest sites discovered by researchers in Ohio, the Big Thicket area of Texas, Washington State and even Klawock Lake, Alaska. The interesting thing about all these seeming nest sites is that the nests appear to be made with local vegetation that has been snapped off and then woven together into a construct similar to that in which gorillas or bears sleep. Only, gorillas and bears do not weave—people do.

It is possible that some of these sites could simply be the product of humans practicing survival skills, but the sheer number of them mentioned throughout the annals of Sasquatch lore seems to belie the idea that all of these nests were made by humans roughing it in the forest. Additionally, survival students are taught to make shelters that are small and snug in order to conserve heat and protect from the elements. The nests and tree structures found in Sasquatch areas are quite a lot larger than anything a human would need to make.

Again, tree structures and nests are taken as signs that Sasquatch is in an area even if no one has seen the Hairy One. They are classic class B phenomena. With the exception of the Linda Godfrey story where a sighting preceded the discovery of the nest site, we really have no idea what is creating these structures and nests, so we will turn our attention once again to the poltergeist phenomenon to see if some other mysterious force might be at work in our woodlands.

We should, first of all, note that the poltergeist seems more intent on tearing things down than building them up, in most cases. One of the hallmarks of poltergeist activity is the breakage of objects, usually crockery. However, as we delve into various poltergeist cases, we see this energy doing some really interesting things.

Janet and Colin Bord, in their *Modern Mysteries of the World,* noted a case in Pearlsburg, Virginia, where, along with the usual destruction, heavy objects were moved. In one instance, a state trooper who was investigating the disturbance reported that cabinets had been moved that weighed more than two hundred pounds. As we will see in other cases, a poltergeist is quite capable of moving heavy objects and even manipulating them.

Such behaviour is, in fact, quite common in poltergeist cases. The Black Monk poltergeist moved a number of objects, including a heavy dresser, which appeared to dance around the room—the "final straw" on the first day of the event that caused the family members to abandon the house for the evening.

In William Roll's examination of the Olive Hill, Kentucky, poltergeist, we see another clear demonstration of the power of this energy. On 16 December 1968, as Roll followed the family's twelve-year-old son into the household kitchen, the kitchen table "jumped into the air, rotated about 45 degrees, and came to rest on the backs of the chairs that stood around it, with all four legs off the floor". Roll stated emphatically that he had the boy in his line of sight the whole time, and there was no physical way that the son could have been responsible for what the doctor observed.

I find this incident particularly interesting since the force involved seemed to carefully arrange the table and chairs into a structure of sorts.

Hans Holzer gives a detailed account of the journal left by the farmer involved in the Leuthold case mentioned earlier. On 09 December 1960, the farmer writes about the strange case of the disappearing chicken feed. The pot of chicken feed disappeared, so the maid prepared another container. The young woman set the container down to attend to another task, and when she returned, it, too, was missing. The maid duly reported the missing feed to the farmer, who found it ... "hidden behind the stairs, covered with a burlap bag". Again, we see the poltergeist rearranging items to suit its mysterious purpose.

Also in the Black Monk incident, we see an instance where the daughter, Diane, becomes the object of the poltergeist's attention after an amusing incident with the local vicar. Once the energy had convinced the skeptical priest that it was, indeed, quite real, Colin Wilson tells us that the poltergeist seemed intent on proving it meant no real harm.

The energy did this by pinning Diane under several pieces of furniture on the staircase. Wilson makes two interesting observations. First, he tells us that the furniture in question should have crushed Diane and did not. Second, he states that a hall stand and sewing machine that held the girl in place could not be moved until Diane stopped panicking and relaxed. It was as if some energy was holding the items in place.

Colin Wilson also tells the story of the Phelps poltergeist in his epic book on the subject. This incident was one of several historic poltergeist events that Wilson covered and is interesting since the subject of the haunting, a Reverend Phelps, had a strong interest in clairvoyance and mesmerism and had even arranged for a not very successful seance a few days before the poltergeist manifested. One has to wonder if his efforts at spirit communication did not bear delayed fruit.

In any event, the first signs of the unusual happened when the family returned from church, of a Sunday in March 1850, and found their home in complete disarray. They thought that they had been burgled, but as they put the home back together, they found that nothing was missing, including a valuable gold pocket watch, which had been left out on a table.

The family returned to church that evening, but the Reverend stayed behind to keep watch. Wilson comments that the Reverend may have fallen asleep during this duty. Nothing disturbed him, but when the family re-entered the home, they again found the place disturbed. Furniture was scattered, and, oddly, a nightgown and chemise had been laid out carefully on one of the beds with the arms folded across the breast. To complete the picture, socks had been laid at the foot of the gown to give the impression of a person laid out on the bed. Wilson continued his description:

---

In another room clothing and cushions had been used to make various dummies, which were arranged in a tableau, "in attitudes of extreme devotion, some with their foreheads nearly touching the floor", and with open Bibles in front of them. Clearly, the poltergeist had an ironic sense of humour.

---

From this point forward, the Phelps poltergeist seemed to delight in the creation of such scenes. The remarkable thing about the case was the speed with which this energy accomplished its tasks. It was capable of making intricate arrangements in the house, such as the one described above, in a matter of minutes where several women working together might have taken an hour or more.

That this energy was a poltergeist was made clear the next day when the requisite movements of objects, breakage and loud pounding on the walls gave little doubt that the "spirit" was of the noisy variety. In addition, the poltergeist took to breaking glass, destroying seventy-two windowpanes in the home as well as tormenting the young son of the family by stone throwing, tearing his clothes and even snatching him up and dumping him in a cistern of water. The poltergeist also seemed to delight in using the pen, ink, and paper of the Reverend, commenting at one point that the man left fine paper and fine ink around for "the devil" to use.

The poltergeist activity in the Phelps home carried on for some months until the mother and daughter went for a visit to Pennsylvania in the spring of 1851. This event seemed to break the cycle, perhaps because the daughter was one of the apparent focuses in the events.

In all of the above cases, we see the phenomenon arranging the environment to suit itself or, in the Black Monk case, to make a point. One of the characteristics of the poltergeist that we see demonstrated repeatedly is that, while the phenomenon seems to be cagey about being directly observed, it does want to be noticed. If we take the poltergeist and transfer it out of doors, I think that we can infer that altering its environment is exactly the sort of thing that it might do to attract attention without being under the watchful eyes of a human.

It is also emphatically clear that the poltergeist phenomenon is very capable of bending and twisting trees into interesting patterns and even, as we see in some class B cases, shaking trees vigorously. Additionally, the poltergeist would be quite capable of rearranging ground cover to create the nests that are some-times observed. An invisible force would have no trouble performing these actions without being seen, and the poltergeist is a master of performing tricks while the observers are not around or when they are briefly distracted.

This habit of events occurring while the observers are distracted is one of the reasons that researchers are so chary of the poltergeist and why so-called skeptics are always quick to claim that poltergeist phenomena are simply sleight of hand tricks performed by individuals seeking attention.

Nandor Fodor, in the classic Thornton Heath case, went so far as to have the focus of his research brought to the institute where he worked and literally strip-searched by female members of the psychical research group before each spiritualist session that he did with her. Eventually, he discovered that the young woman in question was actually perpetrating fraud in some instances but that some of the apports and mysterious movement of objects seemed quite genuine. As is often the case with Sasquatch, Fodor was left with more questions about the case than answers.

In like manner, the so-called skeptics are quick to dismiss tree structures as either natural tree falls or the work of humans in the forest. Of course, in some cases, they are correct, but the sheer mass of evidence weighs against this theory being the complete explanation of these mysteries just as the sheer mass of class A Sasquatch sightings forces us to admit that people are experiencing something in the wilderness.

We can make the same argument in regard to nests. While some nest sites may, indeed, be the work of bears or moose or even humans, the number of these sites and their proximity to areas where Sasquatch have been seen will make the open-minded observer understand why researchers are sure that nests are a sign of Sasquatch presence.

I think that tree structures and nests are certainly a sign that something beyond the pale is happening in the woodlands of North America. It may also be that these interesting structures are the work of a giant unknown ape or hominid, but they could, just as easily, be the work of a phenomenon that has been recognized by humans for over a millennium: the poltergeist.

We have covered three of the common class B phenomena, but now let's tackle one of the physical signs that researchers see as almost incontrovertible proof of the existence of Sasquatch —tracks.

# 9

## THE EVIDENCE OF TRACKS

AT FIRST GLANCE, it seems hard to argue with the Sasquatch researcher who tells us that proof of the creatures' existence can be found in the numerous tracks and trackways that have been found by many people investigating Sasquatch. Of the class B phenomena, tracks are certainly compelling, and as someone who has taken man-tracking classes, I find tracks interesting.

In this chapter, I am going to look at some cases where tracks were found, and finally, of course, I will show that Sasquatch is not the only mysterious being leaving tracks as a sign of its presence.

In BFRO report #27180, we have an example of a track found in my home province of Ontario. Here is the witness' testimony, slightly edited for punctuation and capitalization.

---

In late June 2007, in the morning, I was mowing my cottage drive. It had rained the night before. In the road I found three prints. Two of the left foot, one of the right. The footprints were about 14 inches long. About

8 [inches] at the widest point. They were shaped ... like a human print. The prints all had 3 clearly shaped toes. The impression was about 2 inches deep. The creature had walked out of my 5-foot ditch to cross the road and took only 3 steps in crossing. Each step was about 4 feet apart. The creature continued in the ditch on the other side, knocking over the tall grass. It went over a log in the ditch that would be easier for a human to go under (due to height across ditch). Many relatives native to St. Joseph Island, Ontario, said it couldn't be a bear and was bigger than anything that lived there. The most interesting point is the depth of prints and the three perfect toes. It [presumably, the ground] normally would be quite hard (tractors don't make a rut), it had rained, and the creature had jumped out of the ditch and landed with one foot, the middle footprint was the best.

---

Even taking into consideration the fact that the ground was softened by rain, a print two inches deep indicates that something with considerable weight walked across this witness' road. Also interesting is the observation that the track bore three perfect toes. Lyle Blackburn, in his excellent book on the Fouke Monster in Arkansas, notes that several of the tracks discovered for that creature were also three-toed.

This three-toed configuration is something not seen on any primate; all primates, including humans, have five toes. While there are many good examples of five-toed Sasquatch tracks, we should bear these three-toed aberrations in mind. We will return to this idea later in the chapter.

BFRO report #31176 gives us another example of a Canadian track find, this time in Manitoba. The witness had gone to pick up their mail at a rural mailbox and decided to take the back roads home. While driving on an unpaved road, the witness noted tracks crossing the road. The subject stopped and looked at the tracks, then called a friend to come and take a look as well. Photos were taken, and casts were made.

The witness observed that it appeared that the track maker came out of a field, walked the side of the road for about an eighth of a mile, and then moved back into the field, where the being crossed back to the road at a forty-five-degree angle. The trackway continued until it was lost in a hard gravel area.

The reporting party observed:

> Tracks were approx. 1/2 inch into the ground. They measured 12 and 3/4 inches long and 6 inches wide. The big toe measured 3 inches long itself. The left foot had a kind of a kink to it. These tracks were in a straight line with approx. a seven foot stride. Some of the pictures showed evidence of toe slippage and all appeared to be flat. These tracks appeared after it had rained the day before.

I could go on listing Canadian cases where tracks have been found, but let us move south of the border for another interesting case.

Renowned cryptozoologist David Weatherly, in an article about Sasquatch on native reserves (reservations) in the *Wood Knocks* journal, gives the interesting tale of a so-called "howler" on the Dine' (Navajo) reservation. The "howler" was experienced in and around the town of Tsaile on the aforementioned reservation. People in the area had been reporting strange vocalizations in the night, and the sounds were so unnerving that talk had turned to Sasquatch.

After a long night of screams, a trackway was discovered that exited Canyon de Muerto and made its way to the edge of Tsaile Lake. The tracks were seen to go into the lake and then come back out, and the trackers noted fish carcasses in the area. The tracks then proceeded north through the desert and into a ditch, which paralleled a nearby road. The track line was finally lost when it turned onto a gravel road, but the entire set of tracks covered an area almost two miles in length.

Local witnesses Johnny and Carol Willeto took their evidence to well-known Sasquatch researcher Cliff Barackman, who investigated. According to Mr. Barackman's website:

Many people in the community saw the footprints, and there was very little doubt as to what left them. When one combines the previous night's frightening vocalizations (a common occurrence that summer), the size of the footprints, the distance between them, the dead fish on the lake shore, and the fact that the track maker was barefoot for over two miles of difficult, prickly, pokey walking, the only conclusion that can be arrived at is that a sasquatch made the prints. For the Navajos seeing these prints, there was no doubt. Soon after the discovery of the footprints, several people in the community observed sasquatches nearby, and their sounds continued to be heard periodically throughout the rest of the season.

Barackman further observes, in his website article, that the track maker might have used the ditch, instead of walking the easier road, in order to maintain cover. If someone had come along the road, it would have been a simple matter of dropping to all fours to avoid being seen. This dedicated researcher also included a Google-map-type photo with arrows drawn in to approximate the track route. Barackman also observed that there were sightings of Sasquatch in the area after this event and vocalizations that preceded it, so it certainly seems that something was haunting the residents of Tsaile over that time period. The important thing to note, though, is that, as is usually the case, no one actually saw this track maker.

If we lift our eyes from Sasquatch research, it quickly becomes apparent that Sasquatch is not the only maker of puzzling tracks in our world. One of the classic events of Fortean studies occurred in the county of Devon (UK) with a mysterious track maker in February of 1855. There had been snow the night before, and when the residents of the county awoke, they were amazed to find a trackway that was said to stretch for somewhere between forty and one hundred miles.

Residents reported (and drew) tracks that appeared to be made by a cloven hoof and observed that nothing seemed to stop the track maker. The tracks made their way through walls and haystacks, and rather than travelling around houses, the tracks simply hopped up on to the roof of the home and went straight on. The prints were even said to lead up to drainpipes four inches in diameter and then pick up on the other end of the pipe.

The appearance of cloven-hoof prints immediately brought to mind the devil, but many sought to explain the case as the prints of field mice, badgers or even an escaped kangaroo. Since there is no real direct evidence of the event, it remains shrouded in historical mystery, but it provides us with a good segue into the world of poltergeist footprints.

We have noted that one of the favourite poltergeist tricks is creating chaos with water. In the Black Monk case, which we have already looked at, the family had issues with spontaneously forming pools of water, a phenomenon that not even the local water board could explain. Toward the end of the manifestations, Mrs. Pritchard, the family's mother, came down the stairs of a morning to discover that the carpet in the hallway was "soaked with water". As she looked, the women noticed strange, huge footprints in the sodden surface.

Colin Wilson, who tells us about the Black Monk case, does not give us much detail about the prints, only to say that they were huge, but I think it is notable that huge footprints are a sign of another mystery we have been examining, and even gave rise to one of its sillier nicknames, Bigfoot.

Colin Wilson's definitive book on the poltergeist also mentions tracks in association with another famous poltergeist case, the Bell Witch of Tennessee. That case has had entire books written about it, but both Wilson and ghost hunter Hans Holzer mention an incident that occurred after the death of John Bell Senior. His son, John Bell Junior, did not suffer at the hands of the noisy spirit as his father had, but he did have one particularly notable interaction with the poltergeist.

The Bell Witch was known to not only destroy things but to speak to the residents of the Bell farm, and, one day, the "spirit" told Bell Junior to go to the window. As Bell watched, the poltergeist is said to have made footprints in the snow, which it claimed would match the boot prints of Bell's late father. The younger Bell did not investigate that claim, but it is clear that the energy that came to be known as the Bell Witch clearly was able to produce a discernible trackway and that it might have been capable of imitating the tracks of a person.

In the days before ghost hunting was accomplished with electronic gadgets, Hans Holzer tells of the use of an old-time ghost-hunting technique that yielded an interesting result.

The home of Carole Trausch in Santa Ana, California, was plagued by paranormal phenomena for some time. Although the episodes did not follow the destructive path of the poltergeist, whatever energy haunted the Trausch home was quite capable of touching people and did so, starting with the children of the family and moving to Carole herself.

As if that were not disturbing enough, the family then began to hear footsteps on the second floor of the house when all the family members were gathered downstairs. These steps seemed to take two forms: the heavier tread of what sounded like an adult and the lighter footfalls of what seemed to be children.

One day, in January of that year, Mrs. Trausch had two neighbours over. The women put the Trausch's youngest child down for a nap only to have the child waken, scared, later in the day. When the ladies went to investigate, they found the bed in the room wrinkled as though someone had been sitting on it. The group had taken pains to straighten out the bedclothes before they put the baby down, and no one had been back upstairs since that time.

The family continued to experience strange events until Mrs. Trausch decided to see if she could get some evidence of whatever was haunting her home. She spread a thin layer of flour on the linoleum floor of one of the upstairs rooms in an effort to track the unseen intruders. The woman had chosen the spot because it was the place where the invisible "children" seemed most likely to make their sounds.

Mrs. Trausch had her two neighbours over again, and it was not long before they again heard the pitter-patter of little feet. Going to investigate, they found:

---

... no child, but the white flour had indeed been touched. There were footmarks in the flour, little feet that seemed unusually small and slender. Next to the prints there was the picture of a flower, as if the child had bent down and finger-painted the flower as a sign of continuing presence. From the footprints, they took the child to be between three and four years of age ... as they stood next to the footprints, there was utter silence around them.

---

Again, we see an unseen presence that is quite capable of leaving footprints and of making another of the sounds associated with Sasquatch—bipedal footsteps. In this case, the sounds were attributed to the ghosts of children, but if we reverse our thinking for a minute and move the "ghosts" outdoors, the footsteps heard by the Trausch family could have easily been interpreted as the work of a curious juvenile Sasquatch.

In the intriguing 1953 encounter of Naomi S., Hans Holzer gives us another example of a seeming ghost leaving visible evidence of its presence. Mrs. S and her husband had purchased their dream home in Lynwood, California, and spent considerable effort renovating the place and bringing the garden back to its former beauty. As Mrs. S was out, tending to the tea roses in the garden, she was approached by an elderly, "fragile" woman "neatly dressed in a faded house dress of another era".

After some initial conversation, the woman declared that she and her husband had built the house. Despite some initial misgivings, Mrs. S warmed to the stranger as she enthused over the garden, and eventually asked her to come in and see the house. The woman was delighted and showed a detailed knowledge of the home that convinced her hostess that she had, indeed, lived in the home.

After an awkward moment when the woman declared that her husband had died in a "large oaken chair that sat next to the fireplace", the visitor brightened again, and the two women spent some time discussing the home before moving back out into the garden. The frail lady declared that she loved the roses the most, and Mrs. S offered to give her some to take home.

Naomi S. turned away to get a tool for clipping the roses, and when she turned back, her visitor was gone. The woman thought that the elderly woman was either rude or had simply been overcome by emotion at the reminder of her former life. Mrs. S could not puzzle out how the woman had disappeared so quickly, but it was obvious that she had been there—her footprints were plainly evident in the soil of the garden.

Anyone familiar with ghost tales knows how this story ends. Mrs. S was having a chat with her neighbour and mentioned her curious visitor and the fact that the woman claimed to have built the house. The neighbour was taken aback since the builder of the house had been dead for years. Additionally, the information that the mysterious visitor provided about her husband's death was confirmed by the neighbour.

Again, a being that had no corporeal form left behind footprints as a memento of its passage.

The late Rosemary Ellen Guiley, in her *Dictionary of Ghosts and Spirits*, tells other stories of track-making haunts. In speaking generally about beliefs regarding the Land of the Dead in indigenous cultures, Guiley notes:

> The Land of the Dead is not always located in the heavens. Perhaps even more often it its located under the earth. The Zulus believe in an underworld, where mountains and rivers and all things are as above. The dead live in villages, and milk their cattle, which are the spirits of the cattle that have been killed on earth, Or, again, the dead may live on the mountain or in the valley on the surface of the earth. One European in Borneo managed to get native guides to take him to the summit of the mountain said to be the region of spirits. He was shown the moss upon which spirits fed and footprints of the ghostly buffaloes that followed them, but his guides refused to spend the night there ...

Note, please, that the ghostly buffalo did not leave ghostly tracks but actual sign that this fellow could see.

There are a number of hauntings recorded in Guiley's encyclopedia that left behind physical evidence, including tracks, but perhaps my American readers will enjoy this little historical tidbit.

The house, though it was actually six-sided, to fit the odd shape of the property, is referred to as the Octagon. Located in Washington, DC, the Octagon is said to be the most haunted home in the area aside from the infamously haunted White House. Built in the early 1800s by Colonel John Tayloe to house his enormous family, the home was the site of not one but two falls down the main staircase that resulted in the death of two of Tayloe's many daughters.

In one incident, a daughter had fallen in love with a British soldier, and her father refused to let the man into his home. The daughter stormed past her father, up the stairs, only to let out a piercing cry and plummet back down the stairs to her death. History cannot tell us whether this death was a tragic accident or a suicide.

In the other accident, one of Tayloe's daughters had eloped and then returned to her father's home to ask his forgiveness. The two met on the stairs, and, apparently, the conversation did not go well. When the angry colonel sought to move his daughter aside and travel up the stairs, she lost her footing and fell to her death.

The house survived the War of 1812 unscathed, and President Madison and his wife Dolly resided there while the White House, which had been burned to the ground, was being rebuilt. The president's wife hosted any number of elegant soirees at the home and is counted amongst the several ghosts said to haunt the place.

There are many phenomena reported in the Octagon, including banging on the walls, moans, screams, sighs, the clanking of swords, phantom food smells, the scent of lilacs (a favourite of Dolly Madison) and, of interest to this book, "the appearance of human footprints in otherwise undisturbed dust".

It is certainly the case that enormous and well-documented foot-prints are found out of doors in areas where others have seen Sasquatch. It may even be the case that some of the footprints left behind are from an unknown animal. We cannot ascertain this, as the track makers are usually long gone when the tracks are found, and, oddly, I am not aware of any cases where a trackway has been used to follow and encounter a Sasquatch.

This leaves open the possibility that some of the tracks being found in wilderness areas are being made by the mysterious energy that I have dubbed the forest poltergeist in the title to this book. Even the most cursory look at the literature of polter-geists and other hauntings with physical evidence shows us that these energies, whatever they are, are quite capable of leaving sign ranging from the cloven-hoofed tracks of the "devil" in Devon to the mystic buffalo of Borneo and a variety of human-appearing footprints in various haunting cases. I see no reason why such an energy, stirring up mischief in the woods, might not leave behind huge, bipedal prints with an enormous stride length.

I will have more to say about the idea of a more paranormal explanation of the seeming Sasquatch tracks in my analysis of this section of the book.

# 10

## SCREAMS IN THE NIGHT

ANOTHER OF THE seemingly telltale signs of the presence of Sasquatch in an area is vocalizations. Anyone interested in the Hairy One is likely to have seen this scene related over and over on the shows and documentaries about Sasquatch.

An intrepid group of Sasquatch field researchers is camped in an area where the Big Man is supposed to have been seen recently. As they sit around a campfire or sit quietly in the darkness, hoping for an appearance by the subject of their expedition, a faint sound is heard in the distance.

"Oh, oh!" One of the researchers exclaims, "I think that was a whoop."

One member of the group cups his hands and gives a long, drawn-out, deep-chested howl. The researchers wait with bated breath to see if a reply will sound from the darkness ...

Sometimes, in this scenario, the researchers do indeed get a howl or other vocalization back, and attempts are made to record the sounds. Trees are knocked and more howls are made in the hopes of drawing their elusive quarry closer. Sometimes, their efforts seem to bear some fruit, and the research group has experiences of closer vocals, wood knocks or even tree shaking. What seldom happens is that these events resolve into a full-on sighting at the time of the class B phenomena.

Once more, the forest poltergeist has made an "appearance" and then melted into the woods.

The vocalizations credited to Sasquatch encompass a huge range. Dr. Jeffrey Meldrum, in his excellent book on the Sasquatch, tells us that "among wildlife species that are relatively solitary, secretive, and widely dispersed, vocalizations play an important role in their natural behaviour ..." Dr. Meldrum further states that the vocal "repertoire" credited to the Hairy One is extensive and includes loud screams, wails, whoops, whistles, grunts, moans, snarls and "tooth popping".

The most common vocalization assigned to Sasquatch is an intense scream that carries for a considerable distance. Researchers and witnesses frequently comment about the volume of these vocals and will often say that they seem to come from a very large animal, something with an expansive chest. Dr. Meldrum notes that male orangutangs drive off other males and attract the attention of sexually receptive females with a booming call that can be heard at a distance of two kilometres, even in the dense woodlands of Borneo and Sumatra.

Dr. Meldrum tells the story of his colleague Dr. Greg Bambanek in *Sasquatch: Legend Meets Science*. Apparently, Dr. Bambanek had an encounter in which something screamed at him in the wilds. The sound was so loud that it made his chest vibrate, and he could feel his pants legs moving from the energy of this sound. It seems that whatever made the noise must have been quite close to the doctor, but he did not report a sighting.

If the reader is interested in hearing some of the sounds attributed to Sasquatch, I highly encourage a visit to the Olympic Project website cited in the bibliography to this text. I would also advise the reader to do a web search on the so-called Sierra Sounds and have a listen to those interesting recordings (you can find samples of the sounds at Ron Morehead's site, listed in the bibliography). This little foray into the world of Sasquatch-related sounds will give the reader more insight into what people are describing in their class B encounters with what can be a very noisy phenomenon.

Interestingly, according to Ken Gerhard in *The Essential Guide to Bigfoot*, the Sierra Sounds have been subjected to analysis by scientists, who state that the sounds were not artificially produced or manipulated. As well, former naval cryptologic linguist R. Scott Nelson's review of the sounds led him to the conclusion that some of the sounds heard may actually be a primitive language.

Podcaster and host of Small Town Monsters documentaries, Shannon LeGro, had a very personal encounter with the maker of sounds in the woods while camping with some other researchers on a property in Washington State.

Amongst the researchers in this party was another well-known podcaster, Wes Germer, of *Sasquatch Chronicles*. Germer had set up his phone to play a recording of a baby crying, a sound that is thought to bring in curious Sasquatch. The recording played on a loop for a "maddening" hour before there seemed to be a response—a soft whoop in the forest.

LeGro describes the scene in her book *Beyond the Fray: Bigfoot*:

We were instantly excited. Another whoop followed close behind that. Soon the whoops became perfectly rhythmic in sets of three and had a singsong quality to them. They also sounded feminine to us.

Forty-five minutes went by with the whoops continuing in the same three-set pattern. Whatever it was, it wasn't far from us or the phone. Then without notice, Wes' phone died, and instantly, the whoops stopped too. We grabbed another phone and started the cries, but the whoops didn't continue. Whatever had been interested had gone away or was now just silent and watching us. We continued on but never heard anything the rest of the night. It is disappointing and disheartening to say that we did record that night, but the sound of the drizzling rain drowned out any other sounds.

---

Amongst class B experiencers, vocalizations are another common event. In BFRO case #65894, a witness staying in a rented cottage on Spectacle Lake in the Madawaska Valley, Ontario, reported howls of an unknown origin.

On the first night of the witness' stay, the group decided to have a bonfire, and around 2200 hours, they heard a series of strange howls. The witness, who had seen a Sasquatch in a previous encounter, assumed that the sounds were made by the Hairy One, but the vocalizations caused considerable excitement amongst the other members of the group. The witnesses ruled out such common cries as those of the wolf, loon, coyote, deer, and moose in trying to discern what they were hearing.

Whatever was making the sounds, they appeared to have carried some volume since the reporting party stated that they seemed to come from beyond the lake and perhaps even beyond the cliffs facing them. The total estimated distance seemed to have been over six hundred fifty metres. The calls came in groups of three or four and went on for over a half hour.

That night, there were other signs often related to Sasquatch presence, including tree limbs cracking and something hitting the side of the cottage in the night. The witness reported that the howling happened again on the second night of their stay and lasted until about 0500 hours, on and off. The witness recorded the calls and sent them along with his witness report. The recording is available on the BFRO website.

In a definite case of "be careful what you ask for", BFRO case #18441 details the testimony of a witness who was out for an overnight campout with a group of friends near Chilliwack, British Columbia. The witness and his group were relaxing and having a few beers next to the Chilliwack River when they decided to have a stroll along the river. The witness had done some reading about Sasquatch sightings in the area and, on a seeming lark, decided to make an attempt at the vocalizations he had heard researchers making on television and the internet. His attempts elicited great hilarity amongst his compatriots until the group heard a return call.

"It was low and sounded like nothing I have heard before," the witness stated. None of his friends could identify the caller either.

The witness continued making calls and getting a response for about ten minutes. "We got one last return call that sounded closer and louder than the rest," this experiencer stated. At that point, the group began to hear breaking branches just inside the tree line. The witness does not outline the group's reaction to the new sounds, but given that he did not want to return to the site the next day, we might conjecture that the group departed the area.

So it is clear that something in the woods is making sounds that people cannot identify. Since these sounds often occur in regions where the Sasquatch has been seen, investigators infer that the Hairy One must be on the prowl. That may be true, but if we again lift our eyes from Sasquatch research and look at the mass of data available on poltergeist and haunting phenomena, we see energies at work capable of making a plethora of vocalizations and sounds.

One of the sounds that Sasquatch is thought to make is a sort of chattering sound that to some witnesses resembles spoken language. Probably the most famous case of "chatter" is found in the afore-mentioned Sierra Sounds, where one of the recordings is often called the Samurai Chatter since it resembles a person(s) speaking indistinctly in Japanese. Interestingly, in *Sasquatch Canada*, I report on the statement of the soldier in the Canadian Forces who heard a similar sound while on security patrol in Northern Ontario.

What I find interesting about this so-called chatter is that there is a long history of spoken language in poltergeist cases.

Catherine Crowe, one of the earliest ghost hunters and one who does not get nearly enough credit, tells of a 1670 poltergeist case in the village of Keppock, near Glasgow, Scotland. This disturbance was marked by the usual stone throwing and mayhem, but in this instance, the energy was recorded as speaking to the witnesses though it was never seen.

Janet and Colin Bord, in *Modern Mysteries of the World*, give several instances where voices were heard in association with other poltergeist phenomena, including a strange case in Leesburg, Florida, where one of the manifestations of the phenomena was phone calls where a voice would demonstrate knowledge of the people in the house while using foul language and making threats. Often, in these cases, the family would be able to see other members of the family in the room as the call was received so that no pranking was possible.

In a less physical haunting, the *Encyclopedia of Ghosts and Spirits* has an entry about Alcatraz, the notorious prison, that details several creepy reports about the prison and its ghosts, including the ghost of legendary gangster Al Capone. One of the things often reported at the prison is the sound of audible ghostly voices.

Guiley also reports the presence of "phantom human voices" in the historical case of the Drummer of Tedworth, a poltergeist with a clear human focus who even took credit for the haunting. In an interesting side note, the man who claimed that he was the cause of the poltergeist phenomenon in Tedworth was actually arrested and tried for witchcraft as the result of his confession and was condemned to transportation (a sentence where the adjudicated is forced to leave the area and often even the country). Given that the disembodied voice in the case was known to shout out "a witch, a witch", one must wonder exactly what was going on in this case.

Speech, or some semblance thereof, is not the only sound that the poltergeist or its ghostly cousins are able to make. The Pritchards, from the Black Monk case, noted that, as the phenomenon became more powerful, they were plagued by all manner of odd noises. At one point, the beleaguered family thought that a cow and some chickens had gained entry to one of the bedrooms. Additionally, "Fred", as the family had named their unseen guest, delighted in making "stertorous breathing noises" outside the bedroom doors at night.

In *The Complete Idiot's Guide to Ghosts and Hauntings*, Tom Ogden mentions that the Drummer of Tedworth case included not only the sound of a beating drum but also "rude animal noises and unintelligible human voices".

Lloyd Auerbach, in his book *ESP, Hauntings, and Poltergeists*, describes a case from a letter that he received after some media coverage he had been involved in. The experiencer in that case describes a number of common poltergeist events, including lights turning on and off, and the cat being levitated, but also mentions that the energy produced a humming noise of varying volumes. One wonders if there were a specific tune involved. Another manifestation of this poltergeist is one that should make Sasquatch researchers take note—the sound of a baby crying when no one was about.

The Leuthold poltergeist described by Hans Holzer produced several different sounds. In his detailed journals, the farmer notes that on 14 December the sound of a bell was clearly heard coming from one of the barns. There was, of course, no bell in that area. Before this occurrence, the maid's sleep had been disturbed by the sound of whistling moving about the farm. Again, a whistling sound in the forest is another of the signs that Sasquatch researchers often take as a sign of their quarry's presence.

Rupert Matthews, in *Poltergeists and Other Hauntings*, lays out his theory of poltergeist progression, noting that these cases seem to follow a distinct pattern of escalation and the descent back to calm. In making his case, Matthews notes that some of the first manifestations of the famous Bell Witch case were the sound of smacking lips and a distinct slurping sound.

Matthews further describes a 1931 case at the remote farmhouse of Doarlish Cashen, involving a family called the Irvings, that manifested some odd noises.

---

The visitation began with the usual low level of activity. In this case it took the form of scurrying noises, accompanied by growling and barking as if some sort of animal was making a home for itself under the floorboards. Now and then there came a loud cracking noise that made the walls shake and the pictures move slightly.

---

After several weeks of these noises, James Irving decided to see if the "animal" under his house would respond to his imitations of wildlife, a talent for which he was well known. The energy under the home accurately copied Irving's fox, hedgehog and badger calls and then went on to mimic several local birds. Eventually, this "haunting" resolved itself into the famous case of Gef the Mongoose. For those interested in the whole of this bizarre case, Matthews outlines the entire event in the above-mentioned book.

As I mentioned, *Poltergeists and Other Hauntings* lays out Matthews' theory of poltergeist case escalation. One of the checkmarks on his list of poltergeist tricks is noises of all sorts. Most common is the banging and knocking that we discussed in an earlier chapter, but Matthews also points out that poltergeists are capable of making a wide variety of sounds, including a case in which a noise near the home was mistaken for cannon fire!

According to the late Rosemary Ellen Guiley, another of the telltale signs of hauntings can be found in one of the earliest recorded ghost stories, that told by Athenodorus, a Greek philosopher of the first century of the Common Era.

"Athenodorus was poor," Guiley writes, "and all he could afford to rent was a house with a horrible reputation for being haunted by the ugly ghost of an old man. The ghost was a chain-clanker. Literally ... The ghost dragged about the house in his leg chains, moaning and scaring away all the tenants."

Happily, this haunting was resolved by the plucky philosopher, who followed the ghost until it pointed out a spot to him. Athenodorus dug up a skeleton from the spot and had the proper burial rites performed, thus ending the haunting.

The trope of the moaning ghost is stereotypical, but in our investigation, we cannot ignore this very commonly seen manifestation of a haunting, as it is yet another disembodied vocalization to add to the impressive repertoire of sounds found in poltergeist and haunting cases.

While I have not shown a poltergeist or any of its less destructive cousins roaring or howling, I did locate one example of an apparition that screamed. In his classic text *Apparitions*, pioneering psychical researcher G. N. M. Tyrell tells of a landowner who parted curtly from his tenant one day.

Later that day, at about 2200 hours, the landlord was standing in his "breakfast-room" when he distinctly heard the sound of his front gate opening and then shutting "with a clap". This sound was followed by the sound of running footsteps on the front walk. The landowner was very conscious of a presence just beyond the window where he stood, and he could hear laboured breathing as though someone were catching their breath after exerting themselves. The witness' testimony continued:

---

Suddenly, like a gunshot, inside, outside, and all around, there broke out the most appalling shriek—a prolonged wail of horror, which seemed to freeze the blood. It was not a single shriek, but more prolonged, commencing in a high key, and then less and less, wailing away towards the north and becoming weaker and weaker as it receded on sobbing pulsations of intense agony ...

---

The witness later found out that his renter had committed suicide on the night of this singular event. The truly bizarre aspect of this experience is that the man's wife was sitting a few feet away and heard absolutely nothing.

It is clear that the poltergeist and its ghostly relations are capable of making a wide variety of noises. It is also clear that these energies, whatever they are, can be excellent mimics. If we transported our poltergeist into an outdoor environment, what sounds do we suppose that an energy already capable of mimicking animals of varying sorts might find to imitate?

The nighttime wilderness is a place full of sounds. If we make a small assumption and grant that the poltergeist is not impaired by physical distance, the options for sounds to mimic become endless. Lions roaring and gorillas vocalizing on the plains and in the rain forests of Africa, jaguars making their peculiar cough in the jungles of the Amazon, wolves and coyotes howling in the forests of North America and so many more. Our mimicking energy would have more than enough fodder for its tricks and could end up producing an interesting variety of unidentifiable sounds.

What about the volume of alleged Sasquatch vocalizations? This trademark of the Hairy One is also seen in poltergeist cases where the sounds associated with these manifestations can be quite loud. It is not uncommon for poltergeist cases to get so noisy that they draw the attention of neighbours and passersby, and I imagine that an energy capable of making a sound like a cannon shot could also bellow a roar loud enough to be felt in the chest and on the clothing.

I think, given the evidence outlined, that it is quite possible to theorize that many of the physical manifestations taken to be signs of the presence of Sasquatch could just as easily be signs of the presence of a poltergeist-type energy in the wilds of North America. In the next chapter, I am going to summarize our findings so far, and then I am going to say a word about apparitions and their place in Sasquatch research before moving on to some thoughts about what the mysterious energy haunting our woodlands might be.

# 11

# SASQUATCH, POLTERGEIST, AND
# SOMETHING MORE

SO FAR, we have looked at the signs that Sasquatch researchers see as indicative of the Hairy One, we have talked about poltergeists and cited some interesting cases, and then we have looked at some of those Sasquatch-presence indicators and compared them to poltergeist and haunting cases. It seems clear that it is just as easy to attribute odd occurrences in the wilds to a poltergeist-type phenomenon as it is to point to Sasquatch as the instigator.

Let's take a moment now and look at some ideas I put forward in *Sasquatch Canada*. In that book, I outlined eleven signs that researchers took to indicate the presence of Sasquatch. I derived those signs from wide reading in the field but suggested that readers who were interested might refer to a book like Ken Gerhard's *The Essential Guide to Bigfoot*. Let's take a moment now and look at those signs in light of what we have learned so far.

One of the things that many researchers cite as pointing to a Sasquatch in the area is an odd silence that develops when the creatures are supposedly around. Researchers note that witnesses often mention this oddity in close encounter sightings of the Big Man. What most researchers either do not know or do not care to remember is that this unnatural quiet, what I call the Silence, is a very common effect seen in all manner of paranormal encounters. My book *Mysteries in the Mist*, for example, is filled with strange encounters that begin with an unsettling silence creeping over an area.

The best-known information on this strangeness comes to us from researcher Jenny Randles, a veteran investigator of UFO experiences and the author of several interesting books. Ms. Randles, in an essay entitled "View from Britain", notes that experiencers of close UFO encounters often claimed that "at the onset of the episode all ambient sounds faded away—bird song, the wind in the trees, distant train noises, etc." Randles found this and other "isolation factor[s]" in so many close encounter cases that she dubbed the phenomenon the Oz Factor.

Randles first began to consider the theory that she called the Oz Factor while investigating a UFO case in which a security guard at an industrial site had a close-range sighting of an object in the sky. One of the precursors to this experience was the Silence that we noted earlier, and, interestingly, when Randles followed up with the other guard on duty in the building that night, not many yards from the man who had the sighting, the other guard had nothing unusual to report.

Considering the size and brilliance of the object seen, Randles considered that others in the area should have seen the UFO as well; however, no other sightings were reported on that night, in that area. The sighting seemed to have been the sole purvey of the one witness, reminding us of the experience of the landowner in the previous chapter who was the only person to hear the horrific scream.

While Randles' research pertains to UFOs, it is quite clear to anyone who reads extensively in the field of high strangeness that the Silence is common to Fortean encounters ranging from the aforementioned UFOs to ghosts and hauntings as well as such well-known "monsters" as the Manwolf. A whole book could be written on this topic, but germane to our discussion, the Silence is clearly mentioned in the Black Monk case as one of the precursors to the disturbances.

The next item on my list was the sound of movement in the brush, typically emphasizing that whatever was moving sounded huge. This item is often combined with another, the sound of bipedal footsteps in the brush. Eyewitnesses to Sasquatch will mention that they felt that some large animal was coming toward them, perhaps a moose, elk, or deer, before the Sasquatch broke cover and revealed itself. Intriguingly, though, this phenomenon, along with the shaking of trees and footsteps, often occurs without a sighting following.

Rupert Matthews, in his book on poltergeists, cites scurrying noises in a house, which are often thought to be animals in the walls, as a first sign of the presence of a poltergeist. Given the power that we have seen in some of these cases, with objects both small and large being moved with ease, the poltergeist phenomenon is more than capable of shaking trees and causing a hullabaloo in the brush.

Remember, too, that in some of the poltergeist cases referenced, loud noises were heard without an obvious source of the noise. In several of the cases that we looked at, sounds, such as dishes smashing or crockery breaking, were heard, but when the witnesses went to investigate, no damage was found. It's entirely possible that this force is simply making sounds in the brush without any physical effect taking place.

Additionally, we have seen that the sound of footsteps is a common haunting sign. Remember the Trausch family, whose story appears in chapter 9. The family experienced two kinds of invisible walkers, one with a heavy tread like that of an adult, and the other described as "the pitter-patter of little feet" (taken to be child ghosts). This is just one of a myriad of examples of this sound in conjunction with haunting phenomena.

One item often noted in class B lore is the intelligence of the "creature". In one case I report in *Sasquatch Canada*, a family returned to their campsite to find that their pots, which had been carefully nested together, had been taken apart and set out individually. Additionally, the creatures' legendary ability to secret itself away from human beings is taken to be a sign of its advanced intelligence. In our discussion of vocalizations, we touched briefly on the thought, based on analysis of the Sierra Sounds, that Sasquatch, or whatever made those sounds, might even have a language, another sure sign of the being's intelligence.

It almost goes without saying that such behaviour is common to poltergeist cases as well. Not only is the poltergeist capable of great destruction, but that energy seems to delight in doing things to confound the humans present. In almost all of the cases we have cited, a poltergeist behaves in a mischievous manner, moving disturbances from one part of the home to another to keep the witnesses in a state of constant confusion. This behaviour, by itself, seems to imply a certain intelligence, but we also see evidence for the intelligence of the phenomenon in such examples as the Black Monk poltergeist's sudden anti-Christian turn after an attempted exorcism. William Roll learned the hard way that the poltergeist phenomenon is intelligent when he told the victims of an incursion that the poltergeist never actually hit people with the items it was throwing around, and was promptly proved wrong when one of said items struck him. No damage was done, but it was clear that the force behind the disturbance was listening and understood what was being said.

Some of the classic behaviours noted in class B encounters are wood knocks and the throwing of objects (usually stones but sometimes items like pinecones). We spent considerable time in chapters 6 and 7 giving examples of both behaviours in the wild and then showing that poltergeists engage in very similar behaviour in the homes that they infest. Recall that rapping on tables actually started the Spiritualist movement, and Rupert Matthews notes steadily increasing knocking and then, at times, pounding on walls as a sign of a poltergeist and the escalation of that phenomenon. My own research tells me that Sasquatch are often accused of smacking the sides of homes, cabins, trailers, and the like though, again, the creature is not seen in many of these cases.

Colin Wilson cites stone throwing as a common poltergeist behaviour, and Guy Lyon Playfair gives several good examples of throwing behaviour in the Enfield poltergeist case as well as noting, along with Wilson, the frequency of stone throwing in poltergeist incursions. I am especially reminded of the photographer from the paper who suffered an impact to his head from a lego thrown at him. While the stones thrown in class B incidents don't usually make contact, more than one witness has noted that the size and velocity of a stone throw, just as in a poltergeist case, could have done serious damage if it had hit someone.

Another indicator of Sasquatch presence in an area is the tree structures and nests that are sometimes located in these areas. To my knowledge, no witness has ever reported seeing a Sasquatch engaged in making structures or nests, but since these items are found in areas where the creatures have been seen, the assumption is that Sasquatch are responsible. I, obviously, do not feel that this assumption is completely valid, and we looked at this phenomenon in chapter 8.

In chapter 8, we saw that the poltergeist is an expert in rearranging its environment to suit itself. In the Phelps case, the energy set up mocking tableaus made of "clothing and cushions" while the Olive Hill, Kentucky, case was highlighted by the phenomenon flipping a dining table and arranging it on top of the dining room chairs, directly in the sight of investigator William Roll. A force that is capable of arranging tableaus and rearranging furniture is certainly able to produce signs like the tree structures and nests found by Sasquatch researchers. While we have no clear example of a poltergeist making a tree structure or building a nest, it does not take much imagination to picture this very intelligent force doing such things if it found itself out in the wilds. Remember, we do not have any visual sighting of Sasquatch engaged in this behaviour either.

One item that I mention in *Sasquatch Canada* that we have not really discussed is examples of prey animals found hanging in the branches of trees in at least one area known for Sasquatch activity. As I point out in my previous text, such behaviour is not known to predators in North America, being more common to big cats like the leopard in Africa.

We have seen that poltergeist energy can move extremely heavy objects, most notably in the Pearisburg, Virginia, case where a state trooper noted that the "spirit" moved objects weighing over two hundred pounds. The Black Monk was also seen to pile heavy furniture on top of the daughter of the house. It does not take much of an imaginative leap to visualize a poltergeist placing a carcass (or anything else it desired) in a tree.

The interesting point in this thinking exercise is: what killed the animal in the first place? It is possible that the animals found hanging in trees were killed by other predators, but one has to wonder if our forest poltergeist is not a little more dangerous than the household variety.

Why would the forest poltergeist act in a more predatory manner than its house-bound brethren? From the many examples in this book and the extensive documentation of poltergeists in psychical research, this phenomenon seems to delight in mischievous, mocking, imitative behaviour. What if our forest poltergeist is actually imitating a rare bipedal primate, either extant or extinct? One of the things that researchers think they know about Sasquatch is that it is a predator. I relate a sighting in *Sasquatch Canada* in which the creature was seen to take a deer, and it is generally thought by researchers that Sasquatch subsist on an omnivorous diet that includes deer, elk and other prey animals. If this is or was true of Sasquatch, then the forest poltergeist might actually be more dangerous than its indoor cousins. I'll have more to say about this imitative trickster idea in the conclusion.

Finally, we come to the crème de la crème of Sasquatch evidence, vocalizations and footprints. I've demonstrated that the poltergeist and other ghostly phenomena are capable of making a wide variety of sounds at varying volumes. I've also shown that the poltergeist and its ghostly relatives can make tracks of varying sorts. I see no reason why, if we transfer the poltergeist energy into an outdoor setting, we would not have a phenomenon capable of not only making the wide variety of vocalizations attributed to Sasquatch but also the three-, four-, five- and other-toed tracks that are the premier sign of the Hairy One.

I find this argument especially compelling when we start talking about tracks with toes numbering other than five since five toes is the magic number for any primate. I will leave it to Dr. Meldrum to explain the mechanics of bipedal locomotion, but suffice to say that such locomotion, without the benefit of a five-toed foot, becomes difficult to explain ... unless our theory is correct. Our forest poltergeist could account for some of the tracks that don't make sense to the flesh and blood researchers.

As I say in *Sasquatch Canada*, the presence of all these signs in our woodlands is evidence that there is something out there, but it is not necessarily evidence that Sasquatch are engaged in an endless game of hide-and-seek with us. I believe witnesses who say that they have seen these creatures. There are simply too many eyewitnesses who have seen a Sasquatch to deny the existence of something in the woods that is giving rise to these sightings. What we cannot do, however, is assume that we know exactly what Sasquatch is or that the force behind class B encounters is the same one responsible for visual sightings.

In *Sasquatch Canada*, I said:

---

It's one thing for a creature to evade the clutches of science when it is assumed extinct or there is no one looking for it but quite another thing for a being to evade the efforts of a dedicated group of humans who are constantly seeking it. I don't think anyone has an exact count of the number of groups and individuals who are actively seeking the Hairy One, but I should think these people would number into the thousands. Add to that the hunters who are constantly roaming the wilds of North America with weapons capable of bringing down a large animal and hikers with high-definition cameras in their phones and we should have something more than blurry images and circumstantial evidence to indicate the existence of Sasquatch.

The Sasquatch researcher will splutter at this, so I will reiterate my earlier point. I believe that (a) witnesses are seeing what they are seeing ... and (b) people in the wilderness are encountering something that is producing all the above signs of Sasquatch activity.

---

I feel that the subject of Sasquatch is much more complex than some researchers want to admit. It is far easier to believe that we are looking for a flesh and blood creature than to acknowledge that there may be a greater mystery here that begs for exploration. The issue, I think, is that those raised in the scientific materialist paradigm have trouble shaking the effects of that education when they come up against a phenomenon that does not lie quietly in that paradigm.

Writers like Stan Gordon, Tim Renner and Joshua Cutchin have done a spectacular job of showing us that high strangeness surrounds the Sasquatch if we are willing to acknowledge it. I dive into some strange cases involving Sasquatch with glowing eyes, witnesses experiencing a telepathic connection with these creatures, vanishing Hairy Ones, and even Sasquatch related to UFOs in the chapter titled "Strange Things" in *Sasquatch Canada*. Additionally, I recount some tales of Sasquatch-like creatures associated with mist, fog, and clouds in my book *Mysteries in the Mist*. If, as I keep saying, we look beyond the Sasquatch silo, we can see that we live in a world full of strangeness and that Sasquatch fits right into that world.

Again, I do not deny that witnesses are seeing what they are seeing. Let's step outside the flesh and blood explanation and look at another aspect of the poltergeist phenomenon that might explain <u>some</u> of the visual sightings of our erstwhile subject —apparitions.

# 12

## APPARITIONS

IF YOU SAY THE WORD "APPARITION" to most people, they will likely have a vague notion of a shadowy figure associated with a haunting—something akin to the animated sheets with holes for the eyes and mouth that we see at Halloween. The reality of the apparition, however, is far different and can actually be mistaken for an organic person or animal by the experiencer.

Lloyd Auerbach, in his book on ESP, haunting and poltergeists, outlines three types of apparitions. The one with which most people are familiar is the apparition of the dead, a more or less solid image of person who has died. Next would be the crisis apparition, a figure that appears to a witness in times of extreme crisis. The most common crisis, of course, is the death of the person represented by the apparition, but there are examples of crisis apparitions appearing when a person has been in an accident or a natural disaster. The third type of apparition is the apparition of the living in which an experiencer sees someone who can be shown to have been in another location at the time.

Parapsychologists have several theories, but let us speak instead about what really constitutes an apparition.

G. N. M. Tyrell, in his classic text on apparitions, outlines several aspects of the apparition that are of interest to us. Perhaps most interesting of these aspects is that the apparition seems to appear in a space of its own. A good example of this, given by Tyrell, is the case of a woman sitting in the Birmingham (UK) Town Hall at a concert with her husband. She felt the icy chill known to paranormal enthusiasts as a sign of a paranormal incursion and then saw her uncle lying in a bed with an appealing look on his face. She commented that it looked as though he were dying. The appearance of this apparition was completely solid, as if the man and his bed had been teleported into the concert hall, but the woman stated that she could still see the orchestra as though it were behind the apparition. As you might expect, the uncle had, in fact, died at about the time that the woman had her vision.

Tyrell argues that one of the aspects of the apparition is that it is non-physical in nature. He notes that the apparition often appears and disappears from locked rooms, vanishes while being watched, sometimes becomes translucent and fades away, and may be seen by some people and not seen by others in the same area. Additionally, apparitions are seen to walk through walls and doors and to pass through physical objects such as furniture. Finally, it is the case that people have put their hands through an apparition and even walked through them.

While the non-physical nature of the apparition is apparent from a broad overview of the cases, it is also true, Tyrell notes, that the perception of an apparition is often extremely lifelike. As I noted above, people often mistake an apparition for a living person, and Tyrell makes several points from his extensive case studies that point to this fact. He notes that apparitions often behave as it they are aware of their surroundings. Also, the apparition often appears as a "material person" would. Light does not pass through the apparition but limns the features exactly as it would for a physical person. The apparition seems to observe personal space, and an intervening object will block a view of the apparition until the vision chooses to move. Finally, an apparition appears with clothes on (in the case of a human apparition, of course). The outfit will be complete and may even include accessories such as walking sticks and hats. Apparitions have also been accompanied by dogs, horses and even carriages.

For a couple of good examples of the lifelike nature of an apparition, let's look at two cases from Celia Green's book *Apparitions*.

In the first case, a woman awakens at about 2130 only to find an unknown man standing at the foot of her bed:

> ... dressed as a naval officer, and with a cap on his head having a projecting peak. The light being in the position which I have indicated, the face was in shadow to me, and the more so that the visitor was leaning upon his arms which rested on the foot-rail of the bedstead. I was too astonished to be afraid, but simply wondered who it could be: and, instantly touching my husband's shoulder ... I said, "Willie, who is this?"

The husband did not reply with his wife's aplomb, shouting at the apparition to explain why it was there. The apparition replied in a "commanding but reproachful" voice, calling the husband's name. The husband leaped out of bed, "as though to attack the man", and watched as the apparition moved toward the wall, at right angles to a lamp. The shade of the naval officer actually blocked the light from the lamp as it moved and then disappeared.

After unlocking the door to the bedroom and doing a search of the entire house, the husband returned to speak with his wife, who feared that they may have seen the spectre of her brother, who was in the navy at the time. The husband assured her that this was not the case; he saw the face of the spectre, and it was the face of his father.

Note, please, that this apparition appeared in a locked room, that it was present enough to throw a shadow as it passed the lamp, and that it was solid enough for the wife to believe she was looking at a person when she first awakened. There was no hint of translucency or indication that the apparition was not solid, until it disappeared. Note, too, that the apparition spoke clearly.

A resident of Oxford, UK, reported another very solid apparition as he travelled from New College to Broad Street in that city.

---

As I came down the road I saw two undergraduates in short gowns, one was sitting on a chestnut coloured horse with white socks, the other was holding the bridle rein with one hand and had the other hand on the horse's neck. I was surprised to see a horse there and took a good look at it. Just as I came near the group another undergraduate on a cycle, with a tennis racket, came round the curve very quickly. I shrank back as I thought there would be a nasty accident, but to my

> surprise the cyclist came through the hindquarters of the horse. Very startled I realised the horse and the young men were no longer there.

---

The percipient notes that this was the only time he had ever seen anything unusual and goes on to give more details of the appearance of the two "students". He also notes that when he made enquiries later, he discovered that the location where he saw the apparition was adjacent to where the riding stables for Oxford had been located years before.

We've shown that an apparition can seem so real to a witness that they are convinced they have seen a live person (or horse). Now let's look at the apparition's relation to the poltergeist phenomenon.

As we noted in chapter 3, Rupert Matthews argues that the poltergeist phenomenon seems to follow a very distinct progression. While I agree with Matthews in general, I would argue that there is a certain subset of cases in which apparitional activity seems to blend into the case.

Matthews states that apparitions in poltergeist cases seem to be "shadowy and fleeting". In his investigation of a case in Ringcroft, UK, a "vague black cloud" was seen in association with the incident, while the Drummer of Tedworth appeared, at times, as an "indistinct black figure". He goes on, however, to discuss such matters as crisis apparitions, which we have seen are associated with emergencies and can be vividly lifelike. We have also seen lifelike apparitions in association with the poltergeist phenomenon.

In chapter 3, we found that the poltergeist of 37 Westgate seemingly took on an appearance toward the end of the disturbance.

In that case, the image seen was of a white-haired man in a long robe. We also saw the Black Monk of Pontrefact take on a visible form in the final stages of that disturbance. That energy assumed the form of a monk dressed in black robes, possibly cueing into local stories of an area monk who did not keep his vows and was hanged for rape.

In the famed Enfield poltergeist case, we see neighbours Vic Nottingham and Mrs. Harper both seeing the apparition of a "grey haired old lady". Guy Playfair, who documented the case, notes that when the two witnesses compared descriptions of their apparitions, they matched perfectly. The only difference is that one witness saw the older woman in the front window of the house, while the other saw her in a back window.

While not a poltergeist case, except in that the spectre in question left footprints, the strange case of Naomi S. in Hans Holzer's *Ghosts* is another good example of a lifelike apparition. As you might remember, in that case, the witness saw and spoke extensively with an older woman who claimed to have been one of the original builders of Naomi's house. Naomi took the older woman through the house and then into the garden of the home, and the ghost disappeared when the householder turned to get a set of shears in the garden, intending to give the visitor some roses to take home with her.

When Naomi S. turned back to her guest, the woman had disappeared. A neighbour later told Naomi that the couple who had originally occupied the home had been dead for several years.

As we have taken this brief survey of the apparition, we have seen that these non-corporeal entities appear very solid and real to the people seeing them, that they are often seen to interact with the witness, and that they have been associated with the poltergeist phenomenon that we have spent so much time looking into. What, the reader may ask, does this have to do with Sasquatch sightings?

I want to make it plain that the following is strictly conjectural—a theory that I derived as I plunged into the world of class B encounters and poltergeists. It is one of many theories to explain some of the many sightings of Sasquatch both here in Canada and elsewhere throughout North America. Personally, I feel that there are several theories of what Sasquatch is that could be true, starting with an actual physical creature and ranging through into more paranormal explanations.

Just as we cannot ignore the sightings of witnesses whose reports resemble those of any person who sees a large animal in the forest, we cannot ignore the testimony of witnesses who have seen these creatures disappear or experienced telepathic communication with them. For those who are not familiar with such experiences, there is a small sample of Canadian strangeness in *Sasquatch Canada* and a much fuller reckoning of the high strangeness that follows these creatures in Tim Renner and Joshua Cutchin's *Where the Footprints End* series.

Having said that, let's turn our attention back to the class B / poltergeist interface. We established in chapter 11 that the energy that produces poltergeist activity is quite capable of producing the wide variety of class B encounter phenomena. If we posit that there is a "species" of poltergeist that lives in the wild lands of North America and that this energy mimics the habits of its house-dwelling relations, then we need to talk about Rupert Matthews' theory of poltergeist progression.

The fact is that such a progression is a little harder to document in the outdoor setting. For one thing, many of the incidents that compose a class B episode have already happened before they are discovered. Track evidence, structures and nests fall into this category. While they are strange, the witness does not feel any immediate threat and can continue on their way after documenting their find.

With other phenomena associated with the class B phenomenon, however, there is a definite sense of foreboding. Unlike a home, where the witnesses are unwilling or even unable to leave, the outdoors setting provides an opportunity for escape when things start to get overly strange. While many class B encounters simply amount to a few tree knocks or some howls from an unknown animal in the distance, others become up close and personal. The difference is that, in a case where, for example, stones are being thrown, the camper or hiker has the choice to leave the area. As we have seen, many people do opt to either move their campsite or leave the wilderness altogether.

If the forest poltergeist is following a similar progression to its house-dwelling siblings, people may be dropping into that progression at various points along the spectrum. Remember that the progression starts with small noises that could easily be passed off as local wildlife scurrying in the brush. Later aspects of the progression, such as knockings and vocalizations, would not go unnoticed, and a forest poltergeist in the height of its progression, with violent activity and apparitions, would get the attention of even the most seasoned outdoorsperson. This would be especially true if that activity were accompanied by an apparition that resembled a massive, bipedal ape or hominid.

This idea of progression could account for why some class B encounters seem to be relatively benign, while others are frightening enough to drive even seasoned folks out of the woods.

As we have seen, the question then seems to be: why would the forest poltergeist choose to mimic an animal that is not supposed to exist? Why not, instead, choose to mimic a bear, wolf, mountain lion or some other creature perceived by many to be dangerous.

I believe the answer lies in a behaviour that we have seen over and over again in poltergeist cases; this energy likes to shock and perhaps even frighten people. If there is an actual physical Sasquatch lurking in the woods of North America, what better creature to mimic? While sighting a wild predator can certainly give a person pause, an encounter with a Sasquatch or what the witness perceives to be a Sasquatch in a class B incident will almost certainly be shocking. Such an experience, whether a visual sighting or class B disturbance, as has been noted over and over in a variety of sources, can set the witness back since they are seeing or experiencing something they have been told does not exist. One has only to listen to the plethora of Sasquatch podcasts to see this shock factor in action, making even seasoned outdoors-people chary of the woods.

It may be that the poltergeist is mimicking something that existed at one time. We know, for example, that there was a giant, possibly bipedal, ape living in areas of China that went extinct 300,000 years ago—a drop in the geological-time-scale bucket. *Gigantopithecus blacki* is often cited as a relict species that could explain Sasquatch, but even if *G. blacki* did go extinct, there's no reason why our theoretical forest poltergeist might not choose to keep its memory alive. If the object of this energy's attention is to upset or even traumatize people, then producing an apparition of a giant bipedal ape would certainly serve the purpose.

Finally, it may be that the Sasquatch is not a flesh and blood creature. As I suggested in *Sasquatch Canada*, it may behoove us to look more carefully at indigenous beliefs about this creature.

There is a certain segment of the Native population who believe that Sasquatch is a creature of the Otherworld that has the ability to manifest, physically, in our world and then to move back to its own plane at will. If this happened to be the truth or a truth about these creatures, then this opens a whole other line of inquiry since then we would have to consider what powers such a creature might have. It may be this more paranormal version of Sasquatch is actually the source of these disturbances in the woods, and this is a subject that we will return to in chapters to come.

We have now looked at what constitutes a class B encounter as well as introducing the reader to the poltergeist. We have looked at a couple of well-known poltergeist cases and then compared the various elements of class B incidents with the actions of poltergeist phenomena through several chapters. Finally, we have looked at what an apparition is, some theories about apparitions, and proposed a theory of Sasquatch sightings that may have nothing at all to do with a giant bipedal primate and everything to do with the vast world of spirit that exists beyond our five senses.

What we have not done is conjecture about what the poltergeist and specifically the forest poltergeist actually is. It's time now to remedy that lack and look at some of the energies that could be responsible for all this activity in the woodlands.

# 13
## HUMAN POWERS

IF WE ARE willing to entertain the idea of a certain force or forces wandering our wild lands and creating some of the class B encounters on record, then the question must follow: what is the nature of that force? In the following chapters, I will propose several different ideas from parapsychology and folklore that I feel are good candidates for the forest poltergeist as well as one paranormal theory that I do not feel deserves much attention. As with Sasquatch itself, I am of the opinion that the forest poltergeist is not just one thing and may actually be a combination of things. More on that as we proceed.

The first thing that we must consider is a human source for our mystery. By this, I do not mean to imply that all these events are hoaxes or misinterpretations of events. It is true that people play pranks or deliberately mislead others, and it is also true that humans sometimes make mistakes about what they are experiencing. To try to "explain away" the mass of Sasquatch sightings and class B experiences with this sort of blanket thinking is to deliberately blind oneself to a unique and interesting reality.

Setting aside hoax and misinterpretation, we must acknowledge another great truth that scientific materialism is loath to admit. There is far more to the human being than a random collection of chemicals and water, and under the right circumstances, humans can and do possess powers that remain a mystery to science. Interestingly, according to some in parapsychological circles, strong repressed emotions may be one of the ways in which these wild talents manifest.

In doing research for poltergeist cases, one quickly comes across the concept of recurring spontaneous psychokinesis (RSPK). Both William Roll and Lloyd Auerbach, mentioned earlier in the text and cited in the bibliography, are proponents of this theory, as are other parapsychologists and ghost hunters. RSPK certainly gives us a good jumping-off place for our exploration of the nature of the forest poltergeist.

Let's back up for a moment and discuss psychokinesis (PK), the ability of humans to move objects by mental effort alone. While this ability seems like something right out of the science fiction or horror genre, PK is actually more of a science fact to those who will look at the evidence. Chris Carter, in his excellent book *Science and Psychic Phenomenon*, looks at the major areas of parapsychology and notes that PK, along with telepathy, has been verified in a number of double-blind clinical studies. Carter examines the rigour of those studies in depth and concludes that, if the subject matter were anything other than psychic phenomena, PK and telepathy would be accepted working hypotheses.

While the instances of PK in the studies fell into the realm of micro-PK, subtle changes that are only verifiable in a large-scale clinical trial, we see instances of more large-scale effects in other sources. Ostrander and Schroeder, discussing psychic research behind the Iron Curtain in their 1970 classic, talk about the case of a Russian woman, Nina Kulagina, who was able to separate the yolk of an egg from the white while the egg was encased in a hermetically sealed glass jar. The woman also demonstrated to a Soviet medical doctor that she could speed up his heart rate. In fact, that experiment had to be terminated, as the doctor's heart rate reached dangerous levels.

One might be tempted to think that only special or gifted individuals are able to achieve such feats, but parapsychologists, in the RSPK theory, conjecture that almost any human mind, if subjected to considerable stress, may be capable of spontaneous PK and that such outbursts might move into the realm of macro-PK, effects that are no longer subtle. The parapsychological view of a poltergeist centers around the person whom we mentioned earlier, the focus. This individual is usually noted to be an adolescent or pre-adolescent, but there are instances where a more mature person, subjected to stresses which they could not or would not express, was viewed as the focus.

The theory in these cases is that this central person, placed under the stresses of ordinary development and/or tensions within the household, does not feel free to act out physically so, instead, engages in what Auerbach calls a "psychic temper tantrum". An example of such household stresses would be a family in which the focus is being abused in some way. The focus cannot act against their abuser, so all this repressed emotional energy must find an outlet elsewhere.

As we have seen, the poltergeist is capable of very destructive behaviour, shattering glass and crockery, breaking windows and even, rarely, causing harm to persons about the household. Mostly, however, it seems that the energy just wants to shock or scare people. As we have seen throughout our examination of the poltergeist phenomena, the behaviour can be very similar to a youngster venting their frustration by throwing a tantrum.

When we take ourselves out of doors and look at class B encounters, we see a very similar pattern, where an energy throws things, moves about in the brush, pounds on trees or stones, howls and generally creates a ruckus with the perceived purpose of either revealing its presence, drawing attention to itself, gaining the attention of others of its kind or driving the witness or witnesses from the area. The activity may not be as radical as that of housebound poltergeist cases, but this could be explained by the fact that most people in Sasquatch or class B encounters are not planning an extended stay in the area. The witnesses are typically hunters, fisherfolk, hikers or others transiting through the great outdoors.

Now, let's take a moment and look at a hypothetical situation or two where the forest poltergeist could have a very human source.

In case A, a couple decide to take a wilderness backpacking trip. Perhaps the two are having a rough spot in their relationship and hope that the trip will help bring them back together. Unfortunately, instead of healing their rift, the isolation of the terrain is simply exacerbating the differences that are driving them apart. Nevertheless, one or both of them refuse to admit that there is a problem or even speak about their feelings. According to parapsychologists, this is a situation ripe for spontaneous PK since we have sublimated feelings approaching a boiling point. Sure enough, as the couple set up camp that night, they are pelted with pinecones from a mysterious source.

Puzzled, they make some effort to find whoever is throwing things but fail utterly, instead subjecting themselves to more frustration as they look for the culprit. Eventually, they give up and, after a quiet dinner, retire to their tent. Maybe one partner's attempt to initiate a romantic interlude is rebuffed, adding to the repressed anger between the two, and suddenly tree knocks begin to sound in the forest.

The couple reluctantly unzip their tent and peer out, hearing movement and heavy footsteps in the brush but unable to see anything that is making the noise. Unless the activity really ramps up, the two might make it for a couple of nights, but, eventually, the disturbances around them convince them they are not welcome. They pack up and leave the area, either moving on to another spot or returning home. Those of a more metaphorical bent might even see the entire incident as symbolic of the state of their relationship.

Now, this scenario is entirely fictional, and I don't mean to imply that all hikers or backpackers have dysfunctional relationships. I am simply saying that this is a scenario where the theory of RSPK would apply. Of course, no one considers this, if the couple report their odd encounter, since Sasquatch researchers tend to view things through their own filter: Sasquatch is a flesh and blood creature stalking the wilds of North America. Receiving a report such as the one above, the only acceptable conclusion is that the Hairy One was creating a disturbance near the couple's campsite. After all, bears do not have hands to throw things, and researchers "know" that Sasquatch seem to be attracted to human women.

While this is true, it is also true that there are more things in the paranormal universe than can be dreamt of in some researchers' philosophies, so the "silo" effect keeps researchers from asking questions that might lead to other theories. As Tim Renner and Joshua Cutchin point out in their previously mentioned book, asking a Sasquatch witness if they have ever experienced any other strange events can lead to a whole new discussion. I would go further and say that asking the witness about their relationships or perhaps even doing a stress inventory might yield some very interesting and enlightening results.

Hikers with relationship issues or other areas of tension are one thing, but I think that we also have to look at another group of frequently frustrated people in the outdoors: Sasquatch researchers themselves.

I have heard any number of people interested in the Hairy One comment that, most of the time, you go out into the woods looking for Sasquatch and end up simply having a nice weekend in the wilderness. There are no sightings, no responses to wood knocks or the howls done to draw the creature's attention, no vocalizations, no thrown objects or other behaviour that could be attributed to Sasquatch. Most people will simply shrug their shoulders and say, "We missed the Big Guy this time. Maybe we will have better luck next time," and head home.

But what if, after many trips into the field, a particular set of researchers begin to feel really frustrated? They have spent dozens of hours in search of their elusive quarry, and there have been zero results. They are in a habitat that they "know" is prime ecosystem for the creatures, and there have been sightings or class B encounters in the area, but in trip after trip, nothing seems to happen. They have invested money in night-vision equipment and even infrared cameras, they have equipment for blasting the latest recording of supposed Sasquatch vocalizations, they have made a considerable outlay for the camping equipment to stay comfortably in the wild, and still their efforts are met with nary a wood knock or stone thrown.

To add to the pressure these researchers are under, perhaps there is some conflict at home. All the time and money that has gone into their hobby would not go unnoticed by a spouse or partner, and if that person does not share the researcher's passion for Sasquatch, tension is quite likely to ensue.

Our erstwhile group, loaded with tensions from home and the frustration of not finding any evidence of their elusive cryptid, ventures into the forest once more. As they are sitting around their campfire, discouraged after another uneventful evening spent trying to attract the attention of the local Sasquatch, wondering if their quest is even worth the time and effort that has gone into it, something besides the stew in the pot comes to a boil. All the frustration of their failed efforts coalesces, and, abruptly, a single loud wood knock sounds, not more than one hundred feet from where they sit.

Suddenly galvanized, everyone is on their feet, scrambling for their equipment. Another knock sounds, coming from another direction! There may be more than one creature walking these woods! Perhaps there are sounds of movement in the woods or even stones thrown or a vocalization, but in any event, life is suddenly good, a sense of purpose has been restored, and the researchers are able to go home with tales of the events of that night. They feel justified in continuing their search and have some ammunition for any naysayers on the home front.

Again, this account is purely fictional, and I have nothing but admiration for the people who put themselves out in the woods, looking for the Hairy One on a regular basis. These folks approach their task with a dedication that is not often seen in many walks of life. Still, I know that the lack of findings must be frustrating at times, and this frustration, mixed with the right person or people, could certainly produce an outbreak of RSPK in the woods.

Such an outbreak of RSPK seems to me to be even more likely in the high-pressure circumstances of filming a TV show. In those cases, the principals have a huge investment in terms of both resources to support the filming and maintaining audience interest. These folks are literally in a situation where the failure to produce some tangible result will result in the termination of the show and their present livelihood. If the Hairy One is not obliging in a particular spot or if the conditions of a shoot have been particularly trying, I could easily see their frustration and worry over the future building to an outbreak of spontaneous RSPK. Wood knocking and howls, in this case, are good for business and for the continued success of such programs. The same might be true of some of the phenomena recorded on the ghost-hunting shows on television.

Having broached the topic of the untapped potentials of the human mind, let's go on and look at a couple of other possible sources for our forest poltergeist that stem from or are related to human beings themselves.

# 14
## THOUGHT FORMS

RSPK IS a leading theory for poltergeist phenomena, but I would also like to take a moment to wander down a couple of other seldom explored aspects of the unknown related to humans and their unexplored power. First, we will look at the idea that humans can actually create "ghosts" and those ghosts can have physical effects in the environment. Next, we will examine the notion that some humans have a spirit (besides their own) attached to them, not as a sort of possession but rather as a co-walker in this life.

The most well-known example of the idea that humans can create ghosts is something called the Philip phenomenon detailed for us in John R. Colombo's book *Ghost Stories of Ontario* and other sources. This experiment, conducted by biologist and statistician A. R. G. Owens and his wife, Iris M. Owens, a leader in MENSA, involved a circle of friends who decided to see what would happen if they acted "as if" they were in contact with a spirit from beyond.

The group developed a character whom they named Philip, an English Cavalier at the time of Cromwell, and placed him in a location called Didington Manor. The group sat as if at a seance, and for some time, nothing at all happened. As they were about to give up the experiment, however, (note a certain level of frustration) "Philip" came through with the usual trappings associated with such manifestations: table tipping, knocks on wood and so on. Communication was established with "Philip" through the rapping, and, to everyone's surprise, the "spirit" began revising the backstory that the group had developed for him.

While so-called skeptics fuss about the poor controls for the experiment, those with some experience in the esoteric are not surprised by these results. The magically inclined have been creating thought forms for centuries and, in their book *The Magical Use of Thought Forms,* Dolores Ashcroft-Nowicki and Herbie Brennan lay out how this is accomplished with a strong application of desire, visualization and imagination combined, in their case, with a strong ritual structure that would add further energy to the work.

The result of such actions in one with a trained imagination or a talent for thought forms is an artificial spirit that is, hopefully, programmed to achieve a certain purpose and then dissolve back into the elements. While they are extant, however, thought forms seem to be able to take a seemingly solid form (an apparition, if you will) and to have effects in physical reality if enough concentration is applied in making them.

An example of this occurs in magician Dion Fortune's (Violet Firth) classic book *Psychic Self Defence.* In this case, the formation of the thought form occurred quite by accident.

> I had received serious injury from someone who, at considerable cost to myself, I had disinterestedly helped, and I was sorely tempted to retaliate. Lying on my bed resting one afternoon, I was brooding over my resentment, and while so brooding, drifted towards the borders of sleep. There came to my mind the thought of casting off all restraint and going berserk. The ancient Nordic myths rose before me, and I thought of Fenris, the Wolf-horror of the North. Immediately I felt a curious drawing out sensation from my solar plexus, and there materialised beside me on the bed a large wolf. It was a well-materialised ectoplasmic form. Like Z., it was grey and colourless, and like him, it had weight. I could distinctly feel its back pressing against me as it lay beside me on the bed as a large dog might ...

Note that this "well-materialised ectoplasmic form" was solid enough that Fortune could feel the creature lying next to her. Needless to say, once Fortune realized what she had accidentally done, she sought out the counsel of her teacher and received instruction in how to re-absorb what she had created. This last was done with no little difficulty.

Janet and Stewart Farrar, early practitioners of Wicca, recount another thought-form story in their *Witches Bible Compleat*. Their group, called a coven in Wicca, was very concerned about a seal breeding ground on the Inishkea islands off the coast of Ireland. Fishermen had been known to come ashore and slay the seal pups, whom they saw as creatures that competed with them for the catch. The Farrar's coven created a thought form that they called Mara to protect the seals. The focus of the ritual was a painting of Mara done by one of the group. Later, the Farrars learned that there were reports of a person who resembled Mara walking amongst the seal pups. It seems that, while we have no evidence of physical interaction with its environment, Mara served her/its purpose.

Now, the wolf thought form came forth from the mind of one who was in the process of training in magic and who went on to become one of the most influential voices in early twentieth-century occultism. Likewise, Mara was created by a group of trained occultists who had experience in the creation of these forms. What we see clearly is the application of desire, visualization, and imagination in forming these artificial creations. For more information on what these three terms mean in this context, I strongly suggest reading the Ashcroft-Nowicki book. It is of great interest to anyone interested in the paranormal and will give the Dogman researcher food for thought in its first chapters.

It seems though, that one does not necessarily have to have trained magicians to create a thought form. Alan Moore, the creator of the fictional character John Constantine, claims to have seen his creation walking about in London.

---

I was in Westminster in London ... and I was sitting at a sandwich bar. All of a sudden, up the stairs came John Constantine. It wasn't Sting, it was John Constantine. He was wearing the trench coat, a short cut—he looked —no, he didn't even look exactly like Sting. He looked exactly like John Constantine. He looked at me, stared me straight in the eyes, smiled, nodded almost conspiratorially, and then just walked off around the corner to the other part of the snack bar. I sat there and thought, should I go around that corner and see if he is really there, or should I just eat my sandwich and leave? I opted for the latter; I thought it was the safest. I'm not making any claims to anything, I'm just saying that it happened. Strange little story ...

---

A strange story indeed, and it should be noted that the Constantine character is actually a mage who does battle with arcane forces in the comics. Again, though, we see the triad of desire, visualization and imagination, this time as part of the fire of the creative process, coming together to create something more.

When we enter the Sasquatch field with the triumvirate necessary for the formation of a thought form, we see that such an idea is not so far-fetched. There are certainly a lot of people now with a strong desire to encounter Sasquatch. In addition, the media popularity of the Hairy One has given a sizeable portion of the population a very clear visual image of the creature. Lastly, there are books and magazine articles out there that take this visual image and write its story, discussing the behaviour of Sasquatch in depth (the faculty of imagination). Given the literal obsession of some people in the field, it is quite possible that we humans have created a thought form (or several) that walks our woods, creating class B encounters and perhaps even some of the class A sightings. In other words, a thought form that acts exactly as we expect that Sasquatch will.

How common this is, I will leave up to the reader, but it is certainly an idea to consider, especially given Fortune's very solid wolf. I imagine that, if this creature had been allowed to wander, some interesting tracks and other wolf sign might have been found in the English countryside, and given that Fortune considered the wolf of Ragnarök, the end of the world in Norse myth, some scary encounters might have been had.

While it is quite possible that humans sometimes create artificial spirits that disrupt our wilderness experience, there is another aspect of human powers that we need to examine. Mike Clelland, in his mind-opening book *The Messengers*, provides some intensely interesting commentary on the UFO phenomenon and abduction scenarios. His ideas gave rise to some of my own theories about encounters with the strange.

Briefly, humans, particularly in the Western culture, have lost most of our rites of passage, those important ceremonial events that mark our passage from one stage of life to the next. Rather than embarking on a vision quest as we reach maturity, for example, the modern human gets a driver's license and goes off to college. While a driver's license might be quite practical, it does not, as a vision quest might, give the young person a chance to establish an overarching pattern for their life or an understanding of their place in society. As a side note, sending young people off, after adequate preparation, to quest for a vision might be a good way to give these young ones a direction for their studies.

Since we do not have these rites that move us from one stage of life to another, we are also lacking in another aspect of rites of passage that was vitally important to tribal cultures: the ability to identify those persons who have a special relationship with the spirit world. Rites of passage were important ways for tribal cultures to identify what we would call shaman and begin that person's preparation for a life of service to the tribe.

In my view, the Otherworld may have responded to this lack of identified spirit workers by developing its own set of initiatic experiences. These encounters with the strange, whether UFO experiences, paranormal encounters with ghosts and other spirits, or a "monster" sighting, seem to cause a perception shift in a certain percentage of experiencers. These people are no longer able to view reality in the same way and set off on a path to learn about the Other.

As Clelland posits, these experiences can identify the people who would have become shaman or wise folk in tribal cultures. If we accept this concept of paranormal experiences opening people to the Otherside, then another, related concept could help explain some of our class B encounters.

It is thought, in many animistic cultures, that humans and particularly those open to the world of spirit, have a spirit attached to them as a sort of supernatural assistant. This being is called many things, in many societies, but a good example is the familiar said to attach itself to witches. Orion Foxwood, a well-known modern-day witch and writer on occult topics, tells us, "The familiar spirit is one that teaches, guides, and even empowers the witch. Traditionally, it was common for this spirit to come to the witch in some animal form, but it also comes as a plant, tree, or a variety of other beings."

Foxwood, in his book *The Flame in the Cauldron*, goes on to say that a familiar can be acquired in a number of different ways, including being acquired in an "accidental way" such as through a near-death experience. The familiar may make itself known, as well, during liminal times, such as dusk and dawn, and in liminal places such as "a graveyard, shoreline, haunted woods, or other natural place reputed to be haunted by nature spirits". Graveyards and shorelines, at least, are places where Sasquatch have been visually sighted. I will leave it to the reader to judge what comprises a haunted wood.

Christopher Orapello and Tara-Love McGuire, in *Besom, Stang and Sword*, tell us that a historical witch's familiar was said to use its magic to aid the witch in finding lost objects, identifying criminals, and divining the future. In modern times, familiars are said to act as "protectors or guardians of a particular place dear to their witches. They may also be employed to watch over the body of a witch during acts of soul flight or leaned on for power transfer in spell work". Interestingly, in historical times, the familiar was often said to be a faery, more on that idea in just a moment.

Whatever the provenance of the familiar, it is obvious that this is a powerful energy that attaches itself to the witch. We see similar spirits working with the shaman of indigenous tribes. As we've seen, a familiar can be acquired quite by accident. Is it not possible that some of our class B encounters are the first manifestations of one of these supernatural assistants reaching out to the witness, seeking to establish a working relationship? To someone uninitiated to the world of spirit, such an encounter could be quite frightening. Only in retrospect, as the person digs into an exploration of the Other, might the contact be established.

Interestingly, Orapello and McGuire tell us that the familiar, in historical times, was often said to be a member of the faery species, a group of spirits we will discuss in depth later in these pages. Such a being would make a terrific candidate for our forest poltergeist, but I feel it is incumbent on me to note that the witch's familiar (and those of faery) were said to take a number of different forms. Might it not be possible that some of the Hairy Ones seen in the forest are actually visible manifestations of the witness' spiritual assistant?

Before the reader completely discards these ideas as impossible or nonsensical, I ask you to remember the words of William Shakespeare and remember that "there are more things in heaven and earth ... than are dreamt of in your philosophy". When we move beyond the scientific materialist paradigm, the potentials of the human mind and the magic that works through us are not fully understood. We've already seen that our forest poltergeist may come from psychokinesis raised by repressed human emotions, thought forms that arise as the result of focussed human attention, or even spirits that seek to work with certain human beings in a symbiotic relationship.

Even with all these ideas, there are other candidates to consider for our forest poltergeist. One of those candidates is an energy that was long considered to be a leading candidate for the house-bound poltergeist: the human dead.

# 15

## THE HUMAN DEAD

IN GENERAL, ghosts are considered to be some part of what is left when a human departs the physical plane of existence in the process we call death. Such an idea is hard to explain in the dominant Christian paradigm since a human is supposed to only have one soul, and that soul is supposed to be off for judgement as soon as the person's physical functions cease, or soon thereafter. What is it, then, that is said to be lurking around haunted places? In the Christian paradigm, such events are often attributed to demons, a subject I will take up later.

Other views of the soul and the afterlife make the concept of ghosts seem more reasonable. For example, I recently heard Lonnie Scott, a leader in the inclusive heathen group The Troth, talking about his research into the old Norse concept of the soul. Speaking with his guest Irene Glasse on his podcast, *Weird Web Radio,* Scott outlined the view of modern Norse pagans that the human soul is actually composed of several parts, some of which dissolve at death and others that carry on as ancestors or move to places in the Norse afterlife or, in some cases, remain behind as what we call ghosts.

John Michael Greer, in his very useful work *Monsters: An Investigator's guide to Magical Beings*, gives us another theoretical framework for thinking about ghosts and how they come about. Greer, an experienced Golden Dawn magician and former head of the Ancient Order of Druids in America, talks about the esoteric view of what happens to humans at death, and I think this is a useful idea construct for thinking about this issue.

The process of death, of course, starts with the cessation of biological functions, but according to Greer, this is just the beginning of the death process. Biological death is called the First Death in Greer's work and involves the "separation of the physical body from the other levels of self". This process can be very sudden in the case of violent or traumatic deaths, or it may take place over a period of time when a person has the time to gradually dissolve the links with his or her body during an illness. Those of my readers who have been around someone in the end stages of a long bout with disease will fully understand this notion.

The second phase of the dying process is called the Second Death, and it involves the breakdown of what Greer calls the etheric body. Simply put, the etheric body is the energetic framework upon which the physical body was based. In most circumstances, this breakdown of the etheric form takes about three days, but Greer states that the time depends on the "strength and health of the etheric body itself" and can also be influenced "by the attitude of the dying person". A person who dies with a very vital etheric body and a strong will to live might remain for some time before the dissolution of that energy framework.

Briefly, the Third Death occurs once the etheric body of the individual has dissolved, and what is left moves onto to another plane of existence that magicians and others call the astral. What happens after that varies wildly, dependent on many personal factors, and, as Greer says, really is not relevant to this discussion.

Greer goes on to talk about ghosts as follows:

In terms of ghosts and ghost lore, the Second Death is the critical point, for it's in the interval between the two deaths that ghostly phenomena can occur. The First Death cuts off all conscious connection with the physical body—subtle links between the physical and etheric bodies remain for some time after the First Death, and play a role in some of the phenomena we'll be considering—but the etheric body is more or less intact and can be used freely until it, too, falls away. Like physical bodies, etheric bodies exist in space and time, and etheric senses (which are subtle versions of the physical senses) give the dead the power to be aware of their surroundings. The dead can see and hear, and they can also move around freely, passing through physical matter at will. The dead who are between the two deaths can also affect the physical world in certain ways, and they can be seen by living people who are in certain states of heightened perception.

Trouble occurs for the deceased when they are trapped between the First and Second Deaths for an extended period of time. Greer notes that the most common reason for this to happen is a sudden and violent death coupled with strong negative emotions. In such a case, the person dies with an etheric body that is at or near full strength as opposed to the person who has time in dying and has been slowly losing etheric as well as physical strength.

While such an instance is clearly a way that a spirit can be trapped between the First and Second Deaths, it is not the only way. The annals of psychical research are filled with examples of ghosts who have stayed in an area for reasons ranging from not receiving a proper burial to being afraid of what happens to them when they gave up their etheric form. Regardless of the reason, at any given time, there may be quite a number of earthbound spirits wandering any given area, and, as Greer mentions, these spirits can have certain effects on the physical plane.

And this circles us back to our mysterious force in the forest. We have seen, throughout the book so far, that, while ghosts and poltergeists are considered separately, ghosts sometimes manifest by effecting their physical environment. While these effects are not typically as extreme as those seen in poltergeist incursions, they definitely get the attention of the people who cohabit with them. Greer reports that if you encounter a ghost that makes a request of you, you should try to honour that request. If you cannot, then you should be prepared to defend yourself psychically, as the ghost may try to haunt you or even "attempt violence".

While not technically poltergeists, we have seen examples of ghosts capable of a wide range of activity. As we noted, Spiritualism got its start through the knocking and rapping of spirits in the Fox home. The haunted Octagon House of Washington, DC, played host to a number of phenomena, including banging on the walls, moans, screams, sighs, the clanking of swords ...

and "the appearance of human footprints in otherwise undisturbed dust". Tyrell tells us of people who experienced apparitions that screamed so loudly that they set the person back a step, and, honestly, we have barely touched the surface of the vast documentation of psychical research.

Medium Michelle Belanger, in their book *Haunting Experiences*, tells the story of a ghost that lurked at the top of a treacherous flight of stairs. The spirit did not seem to have the "oomph" to actually push someone but, instead, created a strong sense that it wanted its target to fall. In the circumstance where a spirit can gather enough energy, it is certainly possible for a ghost to push or otherwise physically interact with a person. How many ghost shows have we seen where these sorts of events have allegedly happened?

Belanger, in a YouTube video titled *The Consciousness of Spirits and the Forms of Haunting*, talks at some length about their experiences as a medium and at one point says plainly that some ghosts are not really stuck, they have chosen to stay because they love a certain place. Belanger points out that, if one were to tear such a place down or even engage in extensive renovations, the result could likely be one or more "pissed-off spirits".

Vengeance and improper burial top the list of folkloric reasons for a haunting, according to Belanger. Looking at all the above, a pattern begins to emerge in which the ghosts that are truly interactive with their environment seem to be fuelled by a strong emotion.

What stronger emotions could there be than a love for the wilderness and an absolute rage at its destruction at the hands of careless humans?

Here is another fictional example that might help explain my thinking on this.

Let's call our ghost Josh. Josh was an avid outdoorsman as a living person. He worked hard all his life, so when he got a chance to go on vacation, he loved nothing more than strapping on a backpack and disappearing into his beloved wild lands for a few days or even a few weeks. Josh studied survival, became very minimal in what he carried with him, learned the names of the native plants and what animals lived with him in the woods. Our character was the epitome of the saying "Take nothing but photos; leave nothing but footprints".

When Josh died tragically in an accident on his way to a weekend hike, he was a strapping young man, full of energy, who made the conscious choice to stay in the place that he loved rather than moving on to whatever the afterlife had to offer. After all, what better afterlife could there be than walking the trails of his much-loved woodland? After appearing to his wife to assure her that he was just fine, Josh settled into a peaceful afterlife existence amongst the trees that had been his safe spot in life.

All that changed one day when Josh encountered a logging crew in "his" wood. He watched in horror as the lumbermen felled trees, and that anger galvanized him. Josh's spirit moved from peacefully haunting the wood to becoming a guardian of the forest, and all thought of moving on to some other afterlife left him. From that point forward, Josh resolved to drive anyone he encountered who was abusing "his" woodland out, and he worked to gather the energy to himself to do that.

Class B–style encounter reports began to stack up. Hikers in the area reported feeling watched, having objects thrown at them, and hearing movement in the brush. Investigators may have gone into the area, but as often happens, while there were some strange events, there were no visual sightings of anything, Sasquatch or otherwise, and their equipment detected no unusual heat signatures or night-vision anomalies.

Oddly, the investigators did note that they had trouble keeping the batteries for their equipment charged ...

While we are on the subject of human spirits taking ownership of the land, it is not unknown, in magical circles, for a human being to choose to assume a guardian role for a specific area. Usually, this place is or was sacred to this guardian's people, and that person went through rituals and made a choice to become a part of the sacred land when he or she passed.

Faery Seer R. J. Stewart once described to me his encounter with such a guardian while meditating on a mound in the UK. He was quite clear that, despite the age of this mound and its guardian, the spirit was still very much active and potent. I imagine that such a being could create quite a bit of activity for the unwary outdoorsman who did not approach the place with respect or who, gods forbid, desecrated the guardian's space.

Josh's story is complete fiction, but given this idea of humans assuming guardianship of a place, I feel the story has some plausibility. While I don't feel that human spirits are the best candidates for class B encounters, I do not remove them from consideration since we have seen that they are capable of at least some of the phenomena that are associated with the class B encounters.

The mystery of death does not seem to preclude people from acting on the things that they are passionate about, and it also seems that at least some cultures believed in the ability of certain humans to assume guardianship of a sacred space after the cessation of their physical lives. We will talk, later in the book, about another group of spirits that are good candidates for the class B disturbances and who have strong ties to the human dead.

Before I move into that topic, however, I must deal with another energy in the paranormal world that could certainly create the kinds of effects that would lead to a class B encounter. These spirits pop up much too often in paranormal discourse, and they are used by paranormal TV as a way to drive up jump-scare ratings of ghost shows. In the next section, we will discuss demons. What they are, what they aren't, how these very rare beings manifest, and why I don't think they are a good candidate for our class B encounters.

# 16

## DEMONS

IT IS unfortunate that I have to deal with the subject of demons in this book, but as we have been comparing the class B sightings to poltergeist activity and thinking of those forces that could cause poltergeist activity, it is only a matter of time before a reader or podcaster asks if these disturbances could be caused by demons. The reason for these questions is clear: there is a seeming agreement, amongst some paranormal investigators, that any seemingly hostile act in a haunting case is caused by a demon or demons.

The assumption, from Christian thought and teachings, is that a demon is a fallen angel, cast by God from paradise for the sin of pride, and determined now to make life a literal hell for human beings. This sadly misinformed view is often pushed in paranormal television, which views the paranormal as a sort of horror genre that will only get good ratings when investigations are seen as dangerous and scary. And what better way to make a televised investigation frightening than the introduction of a spirit that is the prime boogie man of Christian belief: the demon? After all, one can't be the heroic saviour, casting holy water and shouting prayers, if there is no force of darkness to battle, and according to TV executives, viewers will not continue to watch a show that shows the real rigours and sometimes boredom of paranormal investigation.

Personally, I disagree with this stance and would love to see more shows that depict real-life investigations, but I digress.

While there is a class of spirits that seems to match the malevolent reputation of the so-called demon, we need to clear up our terminology. The word *demon* derives from the ancient Greek *daimon*. Here's a little quote from my *Phantom Black Dogs* book to explain:

---

The daimon was simply a spirit, thought of as existing between the moon and the earth in Greek cosmology and thus referred to as sublunar.

These spirits were everywhere in the animistic worldview of our pre-Christian forebears. They inhabited all salient features of the land, and it was recognized that some daimon were willing to associate with human beings while others did not care for our race and were to be avoided.

Human beings worked with daimon and the more powerful spirits, which one might think of as gods or goddesses, as [part of] their religious practice before the coming of Christianity.

---

The Christian creed had no place for such spirits and decreed that, if a spirit were not an angel, then it must be a minion of Satan and part of the demonic horde. I respectfully disagree with that stance and, along with most animists of my acquaintance, maintain that there is far more nuance in the world of spirit than is met in the dualistic angels and demons worldview of Christian thought. We humans are a part of a great ecosystem of spirit, which includes all manner of spirits that hold all manner of attitudes about humans. Some spirits are kindly disposed to the featherless bipeds that walk this planet while others take a more neutral attitude and still others bear our kind active hatred.

For the purposes of this discussion, then, I am going to adapt a very narrow definition of the word "demon", and even then, I am not wholly comfortable with using the term. There are people in the world who work with spirits that are called demons and who derive benefit from that work and do not find the "demons" to be all that hostile. Such spirits might be more difficult to work with and demanding, but they are not innately evil. It's also true that some of the spirits labelled demons in the medieval grimoires are simply repurposed pagan gods. Such beings are powerful and may even be capricious, but they do not deserve the title demon.

Unfortunately, we do not have another term that seems to work as well to describe a malevolent spirit that is actively hostile to human beings, so I will, reluctantly, use the term.

Even those spirits who actively bear ill will toward humans are not all demons. I've done a non-public lecture where I described several spirit groups that could account for hostile hauntings and were not demons.

To qualify for the demon title, I would agree with author Michelle Belanger when they say:

> Generally speaking (and certainly for the purposes of this book), demons are agents of disaster and chaos that willfully visit suffering and disease upon mortals. They are not exclusive to Christianity, nor is the concept of demonic possession exclusive to the Christian world-view. Demons are far older than Abrahamic religions, and many of our classic concepts of these antinomian beings have their roots in religious systems that were old before Christianity was even begun.

In an online video that came out around the time the tenth anniversary edition of *The Dictionary of Demons* was released, Belanger further clarified that, in their view, a spirit only qualifies as demonic if:

- The being has never been human (thus ruling out nasty human ghosts).
- The being has a malevolent agenda aimed at human beings.
- The being is self-aware and intelligent.
- The being seems to take a certain glee in the harm it visits on its victims.
- The being has a certain psychic "scent" that will be plain to psychics with experience of these beings and will aid in discernment.

I would add a sixth note—the demonic spirit seems interested in possessing or, at least, obsessing human beings. It's unclear why this is, but the numerous stories of possession and the presence of possession stories in various cultures seems to bear this out.

At this point, the reader may be asking what in the world this has to do with our class B encounters. Honestly, in looking at material on demons, it seems that the vast majority of people writing in the field are concerned with demonic possession and the various stages through which such possessions progress. It was only in looking through some texts on evocation, the magical act of calling spirits, that I began to have some thoughts on this subject.

Steve Savedow, an author writing about the use of the Lesser Key of Solomon, also called the Goetia, tells us about his experience evoking one of these spirits. "Although no visible appearance took form, we were both stricken with a nameless fear." Savedow and his magical partner immediately ceased what they were doing and released the circle that they had been working in, doing multiple banishings to try to clear the presence from their temple space.

Despite multiple attempts to clear the space that night and on successive evenings, it took nearly one hundred repetitions of the rituals designed to remove negative influences before the "astral fog" that permeated the area finally lifted and, along with it, the "dark presence that loomed in the temple". Interestingly, Savedow reports, almost in passing, that visitors to the home noted an "uneasy feeling" (a staple of Sasquatch and other strange encounters) and that there was mild poltergeist activity during the time before the temple returned to normal.

In an interview with *The Columbus Dispatch*, Rev. Vincent Lampert, a Roman Catholic priest who stated that he had performed many exorcisms (the Catholic rite for evicting a demon that has possessed one of the faithful), noted that there are four types of demonic activity. The priest called one of these "vexation". In this type of activity, the victim is subject to physical attack by an unseen entity. Injuries may include cuts, bite marks and bruises.

It seems clear, then, that those forces we might think of as demonic can have some physical effect on their environment; however, it seems to me that, despite what we may see in the movies, these effects are fairly mild. There may be exceptions to this rule, but, regardless, I believe that there are a couple of good reasons why demons are not prime candidates for our wilderness poltergeist.

First, even a quick look at the vast literature of demonology and possession seems to make one thing clear. The demon is a spirit with an overwhelming hatred of human beings, and its method of work is primarily psychological. John Michael Greer, in his book on monsters, notes that the most common way for a demon to gain a foothold in a person's psyche is brooding. Obsessive greed, anger, resentment, or jealousy can attract these spirits and open a person to the influence of the demonic. Note that the demon is most often working on the psyche of a single person.

There have been documented historical cases of possession happening in groups, but there is considerable argument among scholars both secular and religious about whether these cases constituted actual possession. Psycho-social causes of these outbreaks seem a more likely cause of these group "possessions" than a horde of demons terrorizing a group of people. It should also be noted that diseases like ergot poisoning can induce intense experiences that some would interpret as demonic possession, and this natural cause may account for some of the multiple-person possessions seen in history.

While instances of demonic "vexation" do occur, according to the priest above, again, these actions are occurring to a single person. It seems clear that, like the predator that it is, the demon has marked its prey and is circling slowly, looking for opportune times to strike and weaknesses in its prey that may make the hunt more successful.

The behaviour of our forest poltergeist, while often frightening and sometimes clearly designed to drive someone from an area, does not seem to be predatory. Once a person leaves the designated area of the poltergeist's operation, that individual is no longer troubled except by the trauma of the experience. While there have been cases of both poltergeist and class B phenomena following a person, these cases seem to be the exception that proves the rule.

The second feature of demonic influence that seems to militate against their inclusion amongst the causes of the forest poltergeist phenomena relates to the first. If we see the demon as a spirit predator, then it makes sense that these spirits would favour areas of denser human habitation—villages, towns, and cities—rather than the wilderness areas where people are much more spread out. Predators stalk areas where they can find prey, so, in the same manner, the demon should stalk the places of highest human habitation, increasing its chances of finding new victims.

While I suppose that it is possible that a demon might follow an attractive human into the wilds, it seems more likely that the spirit might try to take advantage of the social isolation to further its hold on the person than that it would spend time throwing stones or knocking on trees. While this might startle its intended victim, it seems that causing obsessive thoughts or desires might be a more likely strategy for the demon, even out in the woods.

Again, the forest poltergeist seems to rattle about in order to draw attention to itself, startle or frighten people or, possibly, drive someone from a particular area. This is not behaviour congruent with the intentions of a demon; thus I do not feel that we need to spend much more time considering the demonic.

I will close this section with some advice to those who find themselves in that brooding space that I spoke of earlier. Demons are not as common as the paranormal TV shows would have us believe, but there are spirits out there, demonic or other-wise, that will take advantage of a brooding person, and these "parasites", for want of a better word, can do quite a lot of damage to the human psyche and energetic field.

Do what you must to turn your mind from your obsession. Pray, meditate, do ritual work, see a counsellor, all of the above. Do whatever it takes to turn your mind to healthier and more productive paths. You will be happier, and you will thwart the demonic and any other parasites that might be lurking in the spirit world.

Now that we have had our forced discussion on the demonic, let's take a quick look at a related subject that sometimes comes up in relation to Sasquatch: the Nephilim. While this subject is not directly aligned to the theme of this book, the thought that Sasquatch might be the giants mentioned in Genesis 6:4 is a continuing theme in certain sectors of the Sasquatch research community. This idea is broached as a possible explanation for some of the high strangeness that seems to surround the Hairy One.

The story of these giants, or Nephilim in Hebrew, is given in more detail in the non-canonical texts called the Books of Enoch. These three books relate the story of certain angels who came to earth and, from what we can glean from the text, took a physical form (something not unknown even in the angelology of the Abrahamic faiths). Though technically fallen, and what Christians might consider to be demons, these angels do not seem to fit into the strictly demonic category we have outlined above. Rather, these beings were said to have taught humans many skills ranging from the arts of war to cosmetics. During their tenure on earth, these beings became enamoured of human women, and the women they lay with were said to have borne children. Those children seem to have been known for their great size.

I am honestly not certain how people make the jump from a giant human to a Sasquatch. Presumably there was some inter-breeding of Nephilim with other humans and perhaps a muta-tion or devolution that led to the Sasquatch race. The thing to consider is that if there is a race of giant hairy beings descended from angelic bloodlines, then such a race of beings might have some interesting powers. Those powers could extend to the sorts of manifestations that we have been discussing in this book, in addition to visual sightings of these beings.

While I am not biblically inclined and the non-canonical texts outside of the Bible hold no real appeal to me, I will admit that the Books of Enoch do provide a compelling story, and the idea that beings of the Otherworld may interact physically with human beings is not unknown. I'll have more to say about that idea in the conclusion to this work.

Physical interaction with humans is a firmly held tenet within faery lore, so let's have a look at a class of spirit that actually makes a good candidate for the forest poltergeist. Let's talk about the faery.

# 17

## THE FAIR FOLK

IN MY NOVEL *Hunting the Beast,* the local Sasquatch clan plays a large role in bringing a rogue werewolf to justice. In that fictional account, I placed the Sasquatch amongst the wild fae, faery folk who belonged to neither the Seelie nor the Unseelie Court. The Sasquatch in that book were able to walk into our world, act as physical beings, and then step back into their own world just as easily. To this day, I wonder if I weren't having a psychic moment when I wrote that book.

My dive into the world of Sasquatch, in this book and *Sasquatch Canada,* has increasingly made me believe that there is something far stranger going on in Sasquatchland than some researchers want to believe. While I may not completely discount the idea that there may be an unknown biological that is being spotted by some lucky folks in the wild, a Fortean approach to this subject requires me to look at all the "woo" surrounding Sasquatch and develop some theories.

As I noted in *Sasquatch Canada,* physical beings, like bears and wolves and moose, do not simply disappear in front of witnesses, nor do they have mind-to-mind communication with those experiencers. Such creatures also are not often noted in the presence of that other mystery, the UFO, nor do physical creatures have glowing, self-illuminated eyes (not, emphatically, eye shine, according to the witnesses). Those are just a few of the oddities that I picked up in brief research for *Sasquatch Canada*, and they are a drop in the proverbial bucket when we look at works like *Where the Footprints End* and Stan Gordon's books on high strangeness in Pennsylvania.

When I, as an animist and researcher of the weird for decades, look at this mass of testimony, I cannot help but think, like Jacques Vallee looking at the UFO issue, that modern researchers need to take a breath. Then we need to open some books and look at human folklore to realize, as author and faery expert Morgan Daimler says, that we have been interfacing with a "diverse groupings of beings within folk belief that have always interacted with humans, can be human-seeming, and can interact tangibly with the human world".

The faery, as I spell the word to distinguish them from the saccharine Tinker Bell image that modern culture has foisted on them, have a long history with humankind, and that history has been rife with both blessings and curses depending on the actions and attitudes of the humans involved. While it was possible to get along with "the Good Neighbours", and even to thrive in their presence, the stories relating to "Those Ones" are filled with cautionary tales of what happens when you cross any of the Fair Folk. Note that in this paragraph, I have used three euphemisms for the faery. There are literally dozens of these phrases used to refer indirectly to the fae since it was considered unwise to attract their attention by referring to them by name.

This caution in reference to the faery folk is borne out in the folklore over and over. Daimler tells us that, while the fae are capable of healing physical illness, helping with manual labour, remedying financial difficulties, and removing curses, the list of harm they can inflict is also long. The faery, amongst all their varying tribes, are sticklers for etiquette and privacy, and if a person violates their sense of decorum, that person can be struck blind, given a deformity, be driven mad or even die, often as the result of what we call a stroke.

Interestingly, for our forest poltergeist theory, the faery can also play merry hell with people who cross them in a different and very physical way. Janet Bord, in her interesting book *Fairies: Real Encounters with Little People,* relates one such incident:

> For example, in 1907 the *Coleraine Chronicle* published an account of strange happenings in the house of John M'Laughlin, an elderly farmer living in County Londonderry, Northern Ireland. He cut down a holly bush with which to sweep his chimney, disregarding warnings from his neighbours that the bush was sacred to the fairies. He soon began to regret his folly, when the soot he had buried in the garden found its way mysteriously back into the kitchen. He reburied it; again it returned. Lumps of the soot were found in the kitchen utensils, and it had marked the white walls and broken the crockery. Stones also appeared from nowhere, breaking the windows and other glass indoors.

This was not the end of the farmer's problems.

> A piece of bathbrick [author's note: a predecessor to the scouring pad] in a closed cupboard was, several people maintain, seen by them to hurl itself across the kitchen and smash into seven or eight pieces against the window sash. A stone weighing two pounds, used as a griddle balance, was also observed to dash about. After negotiating two successive corners, it passed through the closed door into the parlour, where it smashed the window and tore a hole in the curtain ...

Stones would appear in the kitchen, seemingly having come through the roof and the ceiling but without making a telltale hole. When the stones were moved outside, they reappeared in the kitchen as if they had a mind of their own. Additionally, the milk vessels in the barn were filled with stones without the aid of human hands.

Nothing could be done for the poor farmer, and eventually, he was forced to abandon the home and seek other lodgings.

In another instance, related by Paul Devereaux in his book *Spirit Roads*, the household of Paddy Baine suffered from "poltergeist-like" disturbances to the extent that Baine consulted the local wise woman. She checked out the building and told the farmer that a corner of his home was encroaching on a faery path, one of the many invisible tracks that the faery use for travelling from one favoured spot to another. Unlike poor M'Laughlin above, Baine was able to do something about his problem. He brought in stone masons to round the encroaching corner of the house, taking it out of the faery path, and the disturbances ceased.

Poltergeist-type activity was even used to determine whether a proposed home site sat on one of these faery paths. As a way of warning the fae of the intention to build a house in a particular spot, one placed four stones at the site in the places where the four corners of the house would be. A smaller stone was then placed on top of each of the larger stones, and the whole was left overnight. If all the stones were in place in the morning, then work could proceed, but if any of the stones were knocked over, the site had to be abandoned.

Katharine Briggs, the English folklorist who preserved so many faery traditions, gives another good example of the physical effects of faery in her book *The Vanishing People*. In the story of the Brownie of Cranshaw Farm, we meet a brownie, a type of faery that tends to live amongst humans, often occupying a home or farm, and if the humans meet certain requirements, such as a food offering, the brownie is quite useful, performing household tasks.

This particular brownie threshed the corn at Cranshaw Farms until the day one of the farmhands made a comment that the brownie was getting lazy and that the corn was not so well mowed and stacked as it had been in previous years. Speaking ill of the fae is one way to earn their ire, and this case was no different.

That night, "a great stamping and muttering was heard in the barn". The brownie was so incensed that he removed every stalk of corn from the barn and pitched it over the Raven Crag, a stone formation two miles from the farm. The brownie destroyed the entire corn crop in this manner and, once its work was done, was never seen again.

Janet Bord, in her text on modern-day faery sightings, relates the tale of a farmer who, around 1910, was set to mow the grass inside "the 4-acre fort of Rathmore between Tralee and Killarney". These "forts" are neolithic sites surrounded by earth banks and are considered by the Irish to be sacred to the fae. The farmer, O'Sullivan, could not get a mowing machine into the area due to the earth banks, so the grass would have to be hand scythed. O'Sullivan, thinking to make things easier on himself, decided that he would remove one of the earth banks so that he could get a mower into the "fort". Intent on this solution, he and his sons brought a horse and cart to begin the excavations.

After a while, the team of men took a break to rest and smoke a pipe. They turned away from the wind to light their pipes, and when they turned back some thirty seconds later, their horse was no longer standing nearby, attached to the cart. Instead, they found the animal some distance away, placidly cropping grass. Some force had, without alerting them, not only separated the horse from the cart without a sound but moved the horse a distance away.

Wisely, the group took this as a sign to desist in their efforts to remove the earth bank. They re-attached the horse to the cart and returned home. I think, in that situation, I might have considered replacing any of the earth bank that had already been moved and leaving a nice food offering to make up for my lapse!

And if we had any doubt about the faery's ability to interact physically with their environment, Janet Bord tells another story of a young man who acted inappropriately in faery sacred space and suffered the consequences. In this case, the site was another small rath, an earthwork about four yards in diameter.

At night, music as if played by silver bagpipes could be heard floating round the hill, and a boy who lay down on the ground one evening to listen to it, at the same time idly picking up lumps of earth and throwing them about him (as boys are wont to do), was suddenly knocked back as if struck a violent blow. He was found lying unconscious, and it was a long time before he came to his senses and behaved normally again, the clear inference being that anyone who dares to desecrate the fairies' sacred ground will be punished by them.

The faery are not just one type of being, and as I have said about the world of spirit in general, some of them are more kindly disposed to humans than others, thus the Scottish idea of Seelie and Unseelie Courts mentioned above, those faery who were inclined to tolerate humans and those who were not. The folklore makes it clear, however, that no faery will accept a slight from human beings and that the consequences of their punishment often bear a marked resemblance to poltergeist phenomena. In fact, more than one of the authors that I have cited above mentions this similarity.

Though there are exceptions, like the brownie and some of the other fae who favour human habitations or places of work (there are even faery that inhabit mines), the faery are generally found in out-of-the-way places. Contrary to belief amongst some New Age and other modern spiritual beliefs, not all faery are nature spirits. According to Daimler, we can say that all nature spirits are faery but not all faery are nature spirits. Many of the fae fall into a category that Daimler and other folklorists call "trooping" fae, that is, they move from place to place throughout the year.

The more solitary fae may tend to remain in one area, but they are free to move about as they please and often will. Faery seer R. J. Stewart once told me that, when some of the Scots were transported to the New World against their will, those who worked with the faery despaired, thinking that they had lost their contacts in the faery realm. For some time, it seemed as though this might be the case, but, eventually, those contacts followed the seers and established themselves in the New World. This might be why the faery lore of places like Newfoundland, Nova Scotia and areas of Appalachia so closely resembles that of the Celtic lands.

So let's look at why the faery races make such a good candidate for our forest poltergeist.

1. The fae are capable of travelling where they will but seem to favour out-of-the-way places and wild lands. In North America, they would have vast swathes of wilderness to claim as their own. In some ways this would remove them from human presence, but it would also make encounters between human outdoorspeople and faery inevitable.

2. The Fair Folk who have established themselves in an area would either not want humans in that area at all or would expect their human guests to behave with a certain decorum. Any breach of that decorum, say throwing trash on the ground, would invoke the ire of these beings. As we have seen, that ire can include everything from throwing things to physical assault.

3. The fae are invisible to most people unless they choose not to be. Those with psychic gifts may feel their presence, but it usually requires some attunement to these beings to be able to see them, and the fae are very

cautious about whom they allow to see them. Despite being invisible, they can certainly affect the physical environment to create "poltergeist-like" effects.

4. No one really knows what the natural form of the fae is; they are notorious, throughout the lore, for changing shape and even assuming animal forms. I see no reason why the Sasquatch could not be one of the forms that they assume. Alternately, as I theorized in my novel, the Sasquatch might actually be a species of fae. This would explain so much of the weirdness that surrounds these creatures as well as making them capable of producing vocalizations, tracks and so forth.

Whether the Sasquatch is actually a faery or not, the presence of the fae in wilderness areas could certainly account for some of the strange class B encounters people experience in the woodlands, and the faery, with their touchy personalities, general reputation for mischief, and tendency to mark some areas as their own, make an excellent candidate for the forest poltergeist.

As I have said repeatedly, however, the faery are just part of a vast ecosystem of spirits that surround us at all times. In our final chapter, let's talk about the Otherworld and what it might contribute to our discussion.

# 18

## THE OTHERWORLD

WE HAVE SEEN that there are at least five paranormal/folkloric explanations for the strange forest encounters that Sasquatch researchers call class B. Some of those experiences could even move the percipient into the class A, visual sighting, realm under the right circumstances.

The fae, for example, are known shape-shifters, and the shapes that they can assume in the folklore range from dogs and horses to seals and birds of various types. Who is to say that there is not a species of fae capable of assuming the shape of a giant, bipedal primate, perhaps even one with different numbers of toes? One of the tropes in faery lore is that, while these beings can assume varied shapes, there is often some flaw (like different numbers of toes) that will distinguish them from the thing they are mimicking.

But even if Sasquatch is not a faery, we cannot rule out a more spiritual explanation for the Hairy One.

I have made no secret of the fact that I am an animist. I feel that we live within a vast ecosystem that includes both biological organisms and spiritual ones and that the interface between these two broad types of beings is extraordinarily complex. The faery that we looked at in the last chapter are a large and well-known segment of that ecosystem, but they are not the sole inhabitants of it.

In meditation I once had what might be called a vision of the spiritual realm. That realm appeared to me as a continuum with spirits that we might recognize and others that would be so alien to us that we would have trouble describing or even visualizing them. Even the Bible tells of angelic beings that the writers had trouble describing. That continuum also contained a range of beings with vastly different attitudes about human beings.

To some spiritual creatures, we are a curiosity, an entertainment that they view with a sense of bemusement, when they acknowledge our existence at all. The vast majority of beings on the spiritual plane do not even acknowledge our existence. Other spiritual beings are actively interested in human development and do their best to assist us along our path. Still others view us as a minor irritant and go out of their way to avoid contact with us, while yet others are actively hostile to our species and everything it represents, often because of our wanton destruction of the earth.

As I surveyed this vast swathe of living beings, I realized, too, that many of them have the ability to visit the earth plane, the realm of physicality where we live. Some are even capable of gathering etheric substance and assuming a more or less solid shape when they come to call, and these beings, who are not necessarily fae, could also account for some portion of class B encounters and perhaps some of the visual sightings as well. This is an idea that folks who are researching "monsters" like the Manwolf might also look into; I believe there is a reason that

Linda Godfrey noted a confluence between sightings of the Manwolf and indigenous mounds.

Now, I happily admit that all of this is what some people would call unverified personal gnosis. However, I am not the only person on the planet who has had similar experiences. I would maintain that shaman and wise folk throughout history have had a very similar experience of the spirit realm. While the content of the spiritual realm may be seen to vary wildly from culture to culture, it is clear that shamanic cultures believed in and worked with a vast panoply of spirits. I believe that it behooves us to listen to the voices of those who have walked in those worlds.

It is far too easy for those of us raised with the scientific materialist perspective to dismiss these spiritual voyagers as quaint relics of a distant past, interesting only from an anthropological perspective, or, worse yet, as simply misinformed, mistaken or mentally ill. If we open our minds, even a crack, to what these people have known and passed on in their traditions for millennia, then we discover a strange new world where anything can and does happen. And in this strange new world, it is quite possible for creatures of the Otherside to visit us and have a physical effect on their environment.

If Sasquatch is not a fae, then an alternate view might be that it is such a creature, moving freely from the Otherside into our realm and back, sometimes choosing to take a solid form and other times simply manifesting as an energy quite capable of knocking on wood, throwing stones, rearranging its environment, making tracks, vocalizing and all the other woodland signs that comprise a class B encounter.

An interesting idea, when we consider the idea of Sasquatch as an Otherworld creature that manifests in this plane, is the idea of perception. Every moment of every day, our brains are working to gather input, filter that input and present us with a cogent picture of "reality" that will get us through our days. Different people have different perceptions of what should be the same thing. Many of us have likely had a discussion with a friend or partner who maintained that an object was one colour while we maintained that it was another.

If our perceptions differ in such small things, imagine what our brains might do if presented with a spiritual energy that was completely foreign to us, something for which we had no clear referent. It may be that our brains interpret this spiritual being as a giant bipedal primate simply because that is the closest that our brain can come to providing an interpretation.

It may also be that such a spiritual being has some access to our brains or perhaps even to the collective unconscious of Jung's theories and assumes the shape of what Jung would call an archetype, one of the great images housed in that collective unconscious. It is certainly true that humankind has formed the image of the wild man over the millennia and that, in recent years, that image has been honed into the image of Sasquatch. Our theoretical visitor from the Otherworld, looking for a form for itself while on our plane, might latch on to this strong image in the human field and manifest it.

In the same manner, this might be the reason for sudden upticks in other paranormal/cryptid encounters. The Manwolf, for example, could be an Otherworld visitor that takes the form of the werewolf that has been so prevalent in our collective consciousness for centuries.

If we imagine that the Otherworld is a place populated by beings with varying attitudes toward human beings, we might also have an answer for why some of the encounters that people have seem be the work of "Sasquatch" bent on mischief or perhaps seeking to be somewhat irritating, while others seem to be the work of a territorial creature that wants the humans out. It may simply be the difference between having the good fortune to encounter a spirit that tolerates humans or running across a spirit that does not wish to share space with our kind.

Again, this is all conjecture. I cannot prove what I say with a computer, a slide rule or even the ubiquitous EMF meter. There are no mathematical formulae for this sort of thing. If, however, we accept that our world is a far stranger place than we have been led to believe, filled with beings both seen and unseen and some in between, the forest poltergeist becomes more plausible, and a whole new world of mythic creatures opens to us.

Some might argue that we are simply not facing reality by adapting this stance. I would counter that argument by saying that what we take for reality on a day-to-day basis has very little to do with the reality of quantum physics. In that world, our intention can alter the course of an experiment, and light can be both a particle and a wave at the same time. Things in the quantum world seem to be not either/or but both/and. Perhaps our thinking on the strange things and experiences of this world should reflect that.

# AFTERWORD

As I noted in the introduction to this book, I see myself as a Fortean. In other words, I am not interested in just one aspect of the strangeness that surrounds us, but, like Charles Fort and the writers that are beholden to his pioneering work, I am interested in all the weirdness that science tries to brush under the rug. I want to talk about the things that make the materialists cringe and call the topic fringe, when they are not actively questioning the sanity of people who examine these topics.

People report seeing Sasquatch in the woods, but they also report all manner of other odd things. Strange things that defy analysis fall from the sky, people report seeing giant beavers in the Canadian wilderness, and serpentine monsters slither through the depths of many of Canada's bodies of water (see *Canadian Monsters and Mysteries* for some examples of these phenomena). Mysterious mists are reported to manifest strange effects ranging from anti-gravity to bending light and even instantaneous teleportation (see my *Mysteries in the Mist*).

The above are just a handful of the cases I have covered in my own books. I've also included sections on UFOs in *Canadian*

*Monsters and Mysteries*. Unidentified objects in the sky are making a big resurgence as I write this conclusion. Now called UAPs, the objects are making a splash in the news as the US Congress examines these sightings and the US military reluctantly admits that they have no idea what the strange intruders are.

Ghosts and hauntings continue to be a topic that interests people. Not only are ghost hunters featured on a variety of TV shows, some better than others, but research into the afterlife and specifically near-death experiences is getting some limited scientific attention. My own research into the phantom black dog, mentioned in the introduction, led me to discover that what I thought was a phenomenon localized to the UK and Ireland is actually much more widespread and includes both North and South American sightings of this interesting and sometimes frightening apparition.

My whole proposition, throughout this book, has been the idea that we need to step outside of the research silos and look at the Sasquatch phenomenon in terms of all the strangeness that surrounds us.

Let me be entirely clear. I believe witnesses. If someone tells me that they have seen a Sasquatch, unless there is clear reason to doubt their veracity, I will believe them. I was not there, I did not see what they saw, I did not perceive what they perceived, and I am not going to call someone a liar unless I have hard evidence that they are.

My belief in the witness' account, however, does not mean that I have to jump to the idea that the witness saw a physical creature in the woods any more than someone seeing something strange in the sky proves to me that there are aliens from interstellar space encroaching on our planet. What the witnesses' statements mean is that they saw something, and that something is open to interpretation.

This is even more true of the person who experiences a class B encounter. While I have no doubt that these witnesses experienced what they say they experienced, I do not have to jump to our favourite bipedal primate to explain the strange happenings in the woods. As I've demonstrated, there are several psychic, paranormal and folkloric forces that could be a part of the class B experience. This fact in no way invalidates the witness' experience; in my view, it expands the experience and the mystery of that experience.

As I have said time and again, Sasquatch and the class B encounters associated with Sasquatch do not have to be one thing. There could be a number of explanations for the Hairy One and for the disturbances in the woods that are associated with the creature.

For example, I do not rule out the possibility that there actually is a giant, bipedal primate existing in the forests of North America and, perhaps, throughout the world. Such a creature could certainly explain some of the class B encounters that are experienced, especially in really wild areas like the northern parts of Canada and parts of the Pacific Northwest. Such locales are dense enough to hide such an animal, and the human population density in those areas is such that the creature could more easily hide from humans.

If Sasquatch sightings and class B encounters only occurred in those types of areas, I might be more inclined to go all in on the physical creature theory. The truth, though, is that Sasquatch are seen in places where an intelligent, elusive animal would not venture. A good example of this is the sighting, in *Sasquatch Canada*, of two truckers driving along a major highway in southern Ontario. Somewhere in the area of St. Catharines, a town of over 100,000 people, the drivers witnessed a Sasquatch as they drove over a creek bed. Being seen in that sort of setting is not something one would expect from the creature that is jokingly referred to as the world's champion at hide-and-seek.

One has only to look at the BFRO's extensive sighting database to realize that Sasquatch sightings and class B encounters occur all over the United States and Canada. That database is but one of many catalogs of Sasquatch encounters. Many of those encounters are in wilderness areas, but some are in suburbs, close to large cities and even in prairie and desert areas where there is almost no cover for an animal the purported size of a Sasquatch. Why would our hide-and-seek champ, a beast that is supposedly so elusive that humans have not been able to track it down, be frequenting places where it could so easily be seen?

It may be that Sasquatch are simply too curious for their own good, but if that is the case, then why has no one captured or killed one? There are groups that are actively trying to collect a Sasquatch specimen for science. Why have their efforts failed even when they are staked out in areas of high activity?

When we add in the high strangeness that surrounds some of these sightings, from authors like Stan Gordon, Tim Renner, Joshua Cutchin, and others, then we have to adapt a more flexible mindset for dealing with this phenomenon, a more Fortean mindset that is willing to look outside the box. It may happen that someone eventually brings the body of a Sasquatch to light for scientific examination, and if they do, science may be satisfied and proclaim a new species. I would find this exhilarating, but while a lot of researchers were brushing off their hands and proclaiming the end of the hunt, I would be asking, "But what about ..."

Ignoring the presence of the strange in association with Sasquatch does a disservice to those witnesses who have had encounters where the Hairy One vanished before their eyes, where a solid trackway simply stopped in the middle of a field, where Sasquatch and UFOs were seen in proximity, where the creature was said to have communicated mind to mind with someone, where the Sasquatch was said to be handling an anomalous ball of light or even where the creature was seen with clothes on. A body on a slab or in a cage does not explain these cases or the hundreds of encounters where no animal was seen but mysterious disturbances occurred in the woods.

My point is that at some juncture we must realize that there are things that we cannot explain. I've often said that, if you have a low tolerance for mystery, then you might want to consider a hobby other than Sasquatch research (or UFO or ghost hunting, for that matter). The topic seems to have mystery built in.

As I noted in the introduction, I am interested in a lot of strange lore, and I have tried to keep my finger on the pulse of what was happening with Sasquatch reports. Most of the stories I have seen over time seem to indicate that the witness had seen a physical, biological creature, but every once in a while, I would read an account that set that assertion on its head. As I researched for *Sasquatch Canada*, I looked at dozens of stories that could have been the sighting of any wild animal. I would just get to the point where I was actually starting to believe that Canada was simply home to an unknown primate when I would encounter a story that simply could not be explained by a physical creature.

My tolerance for mystery kept me going. It also allowed me to report on the "wild animal" Sasquatch sightings as well as the stranger cases.

The research for this book has driven home for me, once more, just how strange this world can be. There is no one-size-fits-all theory for the paranormal, any more than there is a unified field theory of physics. We have to take the bits and bobs that we think we know and, like a child learning how to do puzzles, rotate the pieces into something that we think fits only to realize that, if we turn the pieces a whole other way, the puzzle looks completely different. It seems that our puzzle may be three or four or more dimensional and that those pieces may fit together in a number of interesting and exciting ways.

In conclusion, let's arrange the puzzle pieces once more, into a theory that is a favourite of mine:

*In this thought experiment, we can surmise that there is a physical, organic Sasquatch that stalks the deep wilderness areas of North America and, perhaps, other areas of the world. This creature is extremely rare and very averse to human contact, perhaps having learned long ago that humans are unpredictable and dangerous. These giant primates may, out of curiosity, get close to humans occasionally, and when they do, their territorial displays can be quite terrifying.*

*However, because these creatures are so rare, it is simply impossible that they are causing all the class B type disturbances and even the class A sightings that are reported throughout the contiguous forty-eight United States and the provinces of Canada. The person who encounters one of these physical animals is a rare person indeed.*

*So, what, one may ask, are the other witnesses encountering?*

*Folktales throughout the world relate to us tales of a mysterious force that anthropologists have labelled the Trickster. Trickster spirits have different traits in the stories of different cultures, but the one thing that they have in common is mischief. They love to play tricks on other spirits, humans and even gods, and they are not respecters of persons, in any way, shape or form.*

*Let's suppose that a particular trickster spirit takes great delight in startling humans in the wilds. We could even posit that this particular spirit uses the energies that it evokes—fear, bewilderment, even awe and wonder—to maintain its presence in our world. In essence, it is feeding off the emotions that it generates. Now, this trickster knows, of course, about the rare and endangered Sasquatch and decides, at least on some occasions, to use that form to try to get a rise out of the two-legs out in the bush.*

*We have already seen that Otherworld spirits like the fae can assume a physical form when they enter this world, so our trickster has great fun rattling around in the woods, banging on wood, shaking trees, throwing stones and making various strange sounds. It looks for places to leave tracks and places just enough prints and sign, like nests and branch structures, to keep the humans looking for it.*

*At times, our trickster shows itself, assuming the form of our very rare Sasquatch creature, and this really gets the humans going. They pour tonnes of energy into finding the creature, and their frustration at not being able to "bag" one or get "proof" that Sasquatch exists contributes to the trickster's energetic food supply.*

*The process becomes a feedback loop with the trickster delighting in its forest mischief-making and humans providing a ready supply of energy to keep the party going by continuing to chase the spirit. It could even be that the trickster sets up "hot spots" as continual feeding areas since the humans seem to love setting up in these areas and trying to evoke a response from "Sasquatch".*

This is just one of several possible thought experiments I have run in conjunction with the Sasquatch and class B phenomena. Suffice to say that, when we take off the blinders of "this must be a physical, bipedal primate" and look at this phenomenon through Fortean eyes, a multitude of possibilities present themselves.

The forest poltergeist of the title is and will remain a mystery until science loses its materialist paradigm and begins to think outside the Newtonian box. That poltergeist may be any of a number of things outlined in this book. It may be some combination of the elements found in the text, for example, a spirit that is attracted by the spontaneous outbreak of PK described in chapter 13. Our poltergeist may be a type of spirit that we have not outlined, or it may be the trickster as we have set forth in this conclusion.

While I have strong doubts about Sasquatch and the class B phenomena being related to extraterrestrial intelligences, this has more to do with my doubts about such intelligences visiting this planet than any opposition to the idea that some of our strangeness could come from "another world". In my view, that other world is more likely to be the Otherworld of spirit than it is another planet in our galaxy or another.

In looking back over this text, I realize that we have covered a lot of ground in a very short number of pages. I have been immersed in these ideas since I was a child and especially so since I was in my twenties. Almost forty years later, I've had the time and experiences to allow the animistic worldview and its limitless possibilities to settle into my consciousness. If all these crazy powers and spiritual beings seem a bit much to the reader as you finish this book, I ask your indulgence.

Don't cast anything aside. Just sit with the ideas and concepts in this book. Let your tolerance for mystery build and then think about these things "as if" they might be true. You might be surprised where your own thoughts, ideas and meditations take you.

———

If you took pleasure in this book, check out W.T. Watson's last book *Sasquatch Canada: Beyond British Columbia*.

Enjoy this excerpt from *Sasquatch Canada*:

## CHAPTER 1: ALBERTA

I chose to begin our tour of Sasquatch sightings in Alberta for two reasons. One is that I am inclined to organize things alphabetically when I can. The other is that there is a richness of data to work from, including a whole book written by veteran Sasquatch researcher Thomas Steenburg. Additionally, the Alberta Sasquatch organization maintains a database of sightings, as does the better-known Bigfoot Field Researchers Organization. Finally, I also found extensive sighting information in newspapers and online articles, all of which demonstrate that Alberta is an active Sasquatch area.

Wikipedia tells us that Alberta is the fourth-largest Canadian province at 661,848 square kilometres (255,541 square miles). The region is extremely diverse, with the northern half of the province covered by boreal forest, while the southwestern boundary is occupied by the Rocky Mountains and their densely forested foothills. In the southeast, one finds a range of prairie environments as well as the so-called badlands, deep canyons from which a number of dinosaur fossils have been retrieved.

As you might expect, the woodlands are home to an astonishing variety of animals, including several large predators, including wolves, grizzly bears, black bears, and mountain lions. From a purely biological viewpoint, if grizzly bears, which can weigh up to 790 pounds, can survive in the wilds of Alberta, then it seems possible that a creature as large as the Sasquatch could do so as well.

David Childress, in his book *Bigfoot Nation: The History of Sasquatch in North America*, gives us the story of one of the earliest Sasquatch encounters in the region.

David Thompson was a British fur trader and explorer who came across strange tracks while walking in an area around what is now Jasper, Alberta. The find was so odd that he recorded it in his diary:

---

I now recur to what I have already noticed in the early part of last winter, when proceeding up the Athabasca River ... we came to the track of a large animal, which measured fourteen inches in length by eight inches in breadth by a tape line. As the snow was about six inches in depth the track was well defined, and we could see it for a full hundred yards from us, this animal was proceeding from north to south. We did not attempt to follow it, we had not the time for it, and the Hunters, eager as they are to follow and shoot every animal, made no attempt to follow this beast, for what could the balls of our fowling guns do against such an animal ... the sight of the track of that large a

> beast staggered me, and I often thought of it, yet never could bring myself to believe such an animal existed, but thought it might be the track of some Monster Bear.

---

I find this account interesting since it gives us insight into the mind of a witness (of sorts). Thompson states that the creature the tracks belonged to was known to the local people, but he always thought that the reports were the result of people's "fondness for the marvellous". It was only upon seeing the gigantic tracks that Thompson was forced to admit that such a creature might just exist, even though he preferred to think that it must simply have been a "Monster Bear".

As we walk through the encounters in this book, we will find quite a number from hunters, hikers, and campers. One wonders how many of those people have seen something they couldn't explain and simply decided that it must have been a "Monster Bear".

While we are on the subject of bears, grizzlies, the largest bears in the region, leave a hind foot track that can range up to eleven inches long and seven inches wide, according to bear-track er.com. The track that Thompson found was three inches longer than this and one inch wider, so it is possible that the trader found a giant bear track. What argues against this, though, is that Thompson makes no mention of the claw marks that would accompany the track of such a bear.

Sean Viala, mentioned more than once in my previous books, gives us a historical account in an article from the *Sasquatch-Canada Virtual Magazine*.

Lake Minnewanka is located in the Banff National Park in Alberta and was the site of an ongoing series of Sasquatch reports in the late 1800s. In 1895, several locals out fishing discovered a track of "gargantuan size" measuring over nineteen inches in length. This find was followed by another, in the winter of 1896, where tracks of a similar size were noted in the snow along the lakeshore. The individual who found the tracks followed them out onto the lake, where a hole had been broken in the ice. This person broke off his tracking when the trail disappeared into the woods.

In late spring of 1896, a trapper out checking his lines saw a large figure moving in the distance. He stated that the creature walked into the woods and had to duck to avoid a tree limb in its path. When the trapper later measured the height of the limb, it was over seven feet from the ground, indicating that whatever he saw was well over seven feet in height.

Two prospectors spotted what they assumed was a large bear in the late summer of 1896 and, being armed, fired on the creature. They were horrified when the animal stood up on two legs and shrieked at them before disappearing into the forest. The two departed with all due haste, and the creature was still shrieking in the woods as they made their retreat.

A similar incident occurred in the early winter of 1897 when, alerted by the barking of dogs, a group of men armed themselves and went out to confront the creature. When the animal was spotted, they opened fire on it, but, once again, it retreated into the woods, screaming as it went.

In 1897, two boys spotted the creature walking along a ridge, and then in fall 1898, a fisherman indulging in his pastime encountered the animal at a range of forty or fifty yards. Again, the human opened fire on what Viala feels was a Sasquatch, and again, the creature disappeared into the forest, emitting "hair raising cries". The fisherman thought he might have hit the beast since blood spatters were found in the area.

The creature just could not seem to stay away from the settlers. In the early winter of 1898, two Irish wolfhounds were found dead, and massive tracks were found in the vicinity and then in spring of 1899, the Sasquatch was sighted again. The creature was seen watching a pair of horses in the corral, and once more, the owner of the cabin where the animal was seen opened fire on the creature, claiming that he hit it three times. The beast fell down but then got back up and made a quick getaway into the woods.

The final sighting of the being in that area occurred in early winter of 1899 as a man on horseback spotted the creature "at a distance". The animal appeared to have a "bad limp" as it walked to the west, and Viala conjectures that this might have been the result of being shot so many times.

In any event, the Sasquatch was not seen in the area again. Given the trigger-happy reaction of the settlers to the creature's presence, I wouldn't blame any creature of the forest for vacating the area.

————

To continue reading *Sasquatch Canada: Beyond British Columbia* please go to https://amzn.to/3Qxy2Mo

# BIBLIOGRAPHY

## PRINT SOURCES

Ashcroft-Nowicki, Dolores, and James Herbert Brennan. *Magical Use of Thought Forms: A Proven System of Mental & Spiritual Empowerment*. Llewellyn Worldwide, 2001.

Auerbach, Loyd. *ESP, Hauntings and Poltergeists: a Parapsychologist Handbook*. Warner Books, 1986.

Belanger, Michelle. *Haunting Experiences: Encounters with the Otherworld*. Llewelyn, 2009.

Belanger, Michelle. *The Dictionary of Demons: Names of the Damned*. Llewellyn, 2021.

Blackburn, Lyle. *The Beast of Boggy Creek: The True story of the Fouke Monster*. Anomalist Books, 2012.

Bord, Janet. *Fairies: Real Encounters with Little People*. Dell, 1998.

Bord, Janet and Colin. *Modern Mysteries of the World*. Grafton Books, 1989.

Briggs, Katharine. *The Vanishing People: A Study of Traditional Fairy Beliefs*. BT Batsford, 1978.

Carter, Chris. *Science and Psychic Phenomena: The Fall of the House of Skeptics*. Simon and Schuster, 2012.

Clelland, Mike. *The Messengers: Owls, Synchronicity and the UFO Abductee*. Richard Dolan Press, 2020.

Colombo, John Robert. *Ghost Stories of Ontario*. Hounslow, 1995.

Cutchin, Joshua and Renner, Timothy. *Where the Footprints End: High Strangeness and the Bigfoot Phenomenon, Vol. 1 and 2*. Independently Published, 2020.

Crowe, Catherine. *The night-side of nature; or, Ghosts and ghost-seers*. JS Redfield, 1850.

Daimler, Morgan. *21st Century Fairy: The Good Folk In The New Millenium (Pagan Portals)*. Moon Books, 2023.

Daimler, Morgan. *Fairies: A Guide to the Celtic Fair Folk*. Moon Books, 2017.

Devereux, Paul. *Spirit Roads : an Exploration of Otherworldly Routes*. Collins & Brown, 2007.

Evans-Wentz, Walter Yeeling. *The Fairy-Faith in Celtic Countries*. University Books, 1966.

# BIBLIOGRAPHY

Farrar, Janet, and Stewart Farrar. *A Witches Bible Compleat*. Magickal Childe Publicattions, 1991.

Fodor, Nandor. *Freud, Jung, and Occultism*. New Hyde Park, NY: University Books, 1971.

Fortune, Dion. *Psychic Self-Defence*. Weiser Books, 2020. (Originally published in 1930).

Foxwood, Orion. *The Flame in the Cauldron*. Red Wheel Weiser, 2015.

Gerhard, Ken. *The Essential Guide to Bigfoot*. Beyond the Fray Publishing, 2020.

Green, Celia Elizabeth. *Apparitions*. Hamilton, 1975.

Greer, John Michael. *Monsters: An Investigator's Guide to Magical Beings*. Llewelyn, 2002.

Gordon, Stan. *Silent Invasion: The Pennsylvania UFO-Bigfoot Casebook*. Stan Gordon Productions, 2010.

Guiley, Rosemary Ellen. *Ghosts and Haunted Places*. Chelsea House Publishers, 2008.

Guiley, Rosemary Ellen. *The Encyclopedia of Ghosts and Spirits*. Facts on File, 2000.

Hansen, George P. *The Trickster and the Paranormal*. Xlibris Corp., 2001.

Holzer, Hans. *Ghosts: True Encounters with the World Beyond*. Black Dog & Leventhal Publishers, Incorporated, 2004.

LeGro, Shannon; Hopf, G. Michael. *Beyond The Fray: Bigfoot*. Beyond The Fray Publishing, 2019.

Matthews, Rupert. *Poltergeists and Other Hauntings*. Chartwell Books, 2009.

Meldrum, Jeff. *Sasquatch: Legend meets Science*. Forge Books, 2007.

Ogden, Tom. *The Complete Idiot's Guide to Ghosts and Hauntings*. Alpha Books, 1999.

Orapello, Christopher; Maguire, Tara-Love. *Besom, Stang & Sword*. Red Wheel Weiser, 2018.

Ostrander, Sheila, and Lynn Schroeder. *Psychic Discoveries: The Iron Curtain Lifted*. Souvenir, 1997.

Playfair, Guy Lyon. *This House is Haunted: The True Story of a Poltergeist*. Stein and Day, 1980.

Playfair, Guy Lyon. *The Indefinite boundary: An Investigation into the relationship between matter and spirit*. St. Martin's Press, 1976.

Powell, Thom. *The Locals: A Contemporary Investigation of the Bigfoot/Sasquatch Phenomenon*. Hancock House, 2003.

Randles, Jenny. "View From Britain". MUFON UFO Journal, June 2004. P. 18 and 19.

Roll, William G. *The Poltergeist*. Cosimo, Inc., 2004.

Savedow, Steve (SS). *Goetic Evocation*. Hadean Press Limited, 2022.

Tyrell, G.N.M. *Apparitions*. David & Charles, 2012. (First edition 1953).

Watson, W.T. *Canadian Monsters and Mysteries*. Beyond the Fray Publishing, 2022.

Watson, W.T. *Hunting the Beast*. Beyond the Fray Publishing, 2021.

Watson, W.T. *Mysteries in the Mist: Mist, Fog and Clouds in the Paranormal*. Beyond the Fray Publishing, 2022.

Watson, W.T. *Phantom Black Dogs: Walkers of the Liminal Way*. Beyond the Fray Publishing, 2021.

Watson, W.T. *Sasquatch Canada: Beyond British Columbia*. Beyond the Fray Publishing, 2023.

Weatherly, David (ed). *Wood Knocks Volume 1: A Journal of Sasquatch Research*. Leprechaun Productions, 2016.

Wilson, Colin. *Poltergeist! A Study in Destructive Haunting*. Putnam, 1982.

# INTERNET RESOURCES

Anonymous. "Report #6579". Bigfoot Field Researchers Organization. August 2002. https://www.bfro.net/GDB/show_report.asp?id=6579

Anonymous. "Report #12100". Bigfoot Field Researchers Organization. 18 Sept, 2001. https://www.bfro.net/GDB/show_report.asp?id=12100

Anonymous, "Report # 14020". Bigfoot Field Researchers Organization. 05 March, 2006. https://www.bfro.net/GDB/show_report.asp?id=14020

Anonymous. "Report #15419". Bigfoot Field Researchers Organization. January 2004. https://www.bfro.net/GDB/show_report.asp?id=15419

Anonymous. "Report #15571". Bigfoot Field Researchers Organization. 20 August 2006. https://www.bfro.net/GDB/show_report.asp?id=15571

Anonymous. "Report #16944". Bigfoot Field Researchers Organization. November 2002. https://www.bfro.net/GDB/show_report.asp?id=16944

Anonymous. "Report #18441". Bigfoot Field Researchers Organization. July 2006. https://www.bfro.net/GDB/show_report.asp?id=18441

Anonymous. "Report #23490". Bigfoot Field Researchers Organization. 01 August 2005. https://www.bfro.net/GDB/show_report.asp?id=23490

Anonymous. "Report #26821". Bigfoot Field Researchers Organization. 17 October 2009. https://www.bfro.net/GDB/show_report.asp?id=26821

Anonymous. "Report #27180". Bigfoot Field Researchers Organization. 24 June 2007. https://www.bfro.net/GDB/show_report.asp?id=27180

Anonymous. "Report #31176". Bigfoot Field Researchers Organization. 29 July 2010. https://www.bfro.net/GDB/show_report.asp?id=31176

Anonymous. "Report #51949". Bigfoot Field Researchers Organization. 11 October 2015. https://www.bfro.net/GDB/show_report.asp?id=51949

Anonymous. "Report #55604". Bigfoot Field Researchers Organization. 16 Sept, 2016. https://www.bfro.net/GDB/show_report.asp?id=55604

Anonymous. "Report # 59610". Bigfoot Field Researchers Organization. 12 June 2018. https://www.bfro.net/GDB/show_report.asp?id=59610

Anonymous. "Report #65894". Bigfoot Field Researchers Organization. 27 July 2020. https://www.bfro.net/GDB/show_report.asp?id=65894

Barackman, Cliff. "2013 Tsaile, Arizona". CliffBarackman.com. Unknown Date. https://cliffbarackman.com/home/projects/footprint-database/database-contents/2013-tsaile-az/

Belanger, Michelle, interviewee. "Demons and the Occult in Media". M Belanger You Tube Channel, unknown date. https://www.youtube.com/watch?v=7wHopQu4bXU&list=PLZouZFdobHQ7PhnlMDaCmiMojz3NmeGtt&index=3

Belanger, Michelle, interviewee. "The Consciousness of Spirits and the Forms of Haunting". M Belanger You Tube Channel, unknown date. https://www.youtube.com/watch?v=h-8mW2VHh3g

Eve, Michele. "The Poltergeist of Westgate Street". Mystical Times Blog. 2023. https://mysticaltimesblog.com/the-poltergeist-of-westgate-street/

Germer, Wes, host. "The Snelgrove Lake Incident". *Sasquatch Chronicles Podcast*. Episode 312, 03 April 2017.

Green, Jules Chin. "Constantine's Writers at DC Comics Keep Meeting Him in Real Life". *ScreenRant*. 27 December 2021. https://screenrant.com/constantine-real-life-alan-moore-dc-comics/

Hajicek, Doug, creator. "Sasquatch Attacks". *Monster Quest*, Season 1, Episode 2, History Channel/Whitewolf Entertainment, 7 Nov. 2007, Accessed 22 July 2022.

King, Danae. "The Catholic Church still practices exorcism". *The Columbus Dispatch*, 28 October 2022. https://www.dispatch.com/story/lifestyle/faith/2022/10/28/curious-about-demonic-possession-and-exorcism-7-things-to-know/69593131007/

Morehead, Ron. "Bigfoot Recordings from the Sierra Sounds". United Date. https://ronmorehead.com

Morris, KB. "The Enfield Poltergeist". Horrified. Unknown Date. https://www.horrifiedmagazine.co.uk/other/the-enfield-poltergeist/

O'Neill, Dennis. "Adaptations of Group Living". Unknown Date. https://www.palomar.edu/anthro/behavior/behave_3.htm

Scott, Lonnie, host. "Irene Glasse Solving Problems with Thor in a Dress, Seidr and Magic." *Weird Web Radio*, episode 87, 12 April 2023. https://www.youtube.com/watch?v=sxoYfZYXIAs

Soule, Richard L. " Sasquatch Tree and Stick Structures". The Nox Gigas Study, unknown date. https://sites.google.com/site/noxgigasstudy/sasquatch-tree-and-stick-structures

Therriault, Ednor. "Call it Yeti, Wendigo, Chuchuna or Sasquatch, you'd better

believe there are believers". Mountain Outlaw, Unknown Date. https://www.
mtoutlaw.com/in-search-of- bigfoot/

Unknown author. "Sasquatch Tree Structures". Sasquatch Investigations of the
Rockies, unknown date. https://sasquatchinvestigations.org/bigfoot-evidence/
sasquatch-tree-stuctures/

Unknown author. "Devil's Footprints". Wikipedia. unknown date. https://en.wiki
pedia.org/wiki/Devil%27s_Footprints, citing primarily Mike Dash's article
for *Forteam Studies* "The Devil's Hoofmarks".

Unknown Author. "Audio Research". The Olympic Project. http://www.
olympicproject.com/audio-research/.

Unknown author. "Gigantopithecus". Wikipedia. Unknown date. https://en.wiki
pedia.org/wiki/Gigantopithecus

Unknown author. "Friday Night Drumming". The Olympic Project. Unknown
date. https://www.olympicproject.com/friday-night-drumming/

# ABOUT THE AUTHOR

Amazon best-selling author W. T. Watson is a coffee addict and writer of both fiction and non-fiction. He infuses his work with his expertise in cryptozoology, monster lore, magic, Forteana and the paranormal. W.T. offers a unique shamanic and magical perspective with over 30 years of exploration in these topics. When he is not writing or reading about monsters, he can be found outdoors allowing his dogs to take him for a walk around his neighbourhood in Kitchener, Ontario. He lives with his spouse, Stacey, in a townhome that would be jammed with books if it weren't for e-readers.

- facebook.com/blackdog60
- x.com/WTWatson2
- instagram.com/curunir60

Hunting The Beast: A Novel

Phantom Black Dogs: Walkers of the Liminal Way

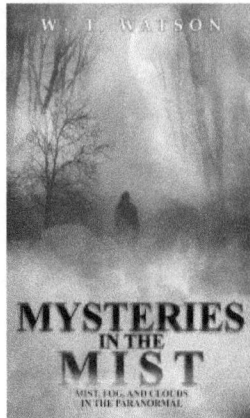

Mysteries in the Mist: Mist, Fog, and Clouds in the Paranormal

Canadian Monsters & Mysteries

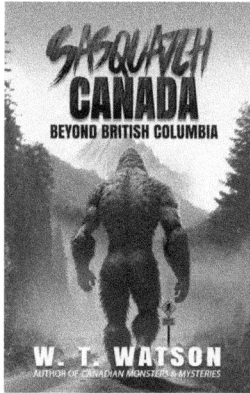

Sasquatch Canada: Beyond British Columbia